RESILIE

A Moment to Reflect, Restore, and Renew

KING JESUS PRESS LLC

RESILIENCE

A MOMENT TO REFLECT, RESTORE, AND RENEW

SHEIRRA MARCI, Ed.D.

ISBN: (Soft cover) 979-8-9886859-2-0

ISBN: (Hard cover) 979-8-9886859-3-7

Author photo courtesy of: Kimazing Photography

DEDICATION

To Alijah, you continue to be the reason why I fight so hard to be the best version of myself. Thank you for trusting me to continue to lead you on this journey through life. Never forget that everything I do in this life is for you. Remember, God has equipped you with everything you need to be successful. All it takes is tapping into the gifts he has placed inside of you. I love you!

To Mother, Momma K, and Daddy, thank you for being a continuous presence in my life. I am extremely grateful that God has blessed me with each of you for more than 40 years. Thank you for believing in me and supporting me through all my accomplishments. It means the world to me. I love you all very much.

To my late grandparents, I love each of you and miss you so much. I know you all would be proud of all the things I have accomplished. Continue to rest well. Until we meet again, I love you all. You all are forever in my heart.

To my siblings - Sergio, Pachess, Shaundra, Amanda, and Scott Jr. - thank you so much for your authentic support. It means so much to me knowing that you all have my back in everything I do. I love you all.

To my nieces and nephews - Katura, Sumarra, Scott III, Serenity, and Samson - I love you all. I am very grateful for the moments I have shared with each of you. I am proud of the individuals you are becoming. Remember, you can do anything you set your heart and mind to do if you just try.

To all my aunties, uncles, and cousins, your love and support mean a lot to me. I love you all.

To my sista circle, close friends, and best friends, thank you for being open, honest, authentic and supportive. I love you all.

To anyone reading this book, I dedicate this book to you. May it touch you in a way you can heal and recover. May it inspire, encourage and uplift you during your journey through life. God is able to do exceeding abundantly above all that we ask or think. Keep the faith!

CONTENTS

INTRODUCTION

Resilience is the ability to recover quickly from challenges, difficulties and tough times. It is the process and outcome of successfully adapting to challenging life experiences. Being resilient means overcoming obstacles from a healthy space, mentally and emotionally. When I think of resilience, three key components come to mind: the ability to connect, control and cope.

To connect means having a strong support system of individuals who commit to standing beside you during the bad times as well as the good. A strong connection helps ensure there is a solid community who is ready to help whenever the need arises. Control is the ability to handle things in a positive, healthy and realistic manner. It is essential to understand there are certain things in life that we cannot control. However, for those things we can control, we must do so adequately. Lastly, coping ensures we execute healthy strategies to manage stress and anxiety. Being able to cope when in disarray is vital.

In the second installment after "Perseverance: A Reflection of Pain, Passion, and Purpose", I am once again transparent, open and honest with my readers. I discuss the challenges, difficulties and tough times I endured as a very young girl who lived with my mom and big sister, and as an adult in my 20s-40s as I shifted, adjusted, and figured things out. When obstacles and challenges arise, resilience is a true testament that with the right support system, resources and authentic faith, things will align as they should. In "Resilience," I share the challenges I faced living in apartment communities and renting from private owners. In my *Home Test* chapter, I discuss experiences I endured with property owners who were filled with greed and those who lacked morals. I touch on having my home sold from under me after being told I could rent for two years. This resulted in losing a friend from high school because she served as the realtor in the deal. I endured inflation in the cost of rent due to the market, making it impossible to save for a home. Finally, I discuss returning to an apartment community that allowed me to budget and save for my forever home.

Next, I discuss the challenges I endured with my finances in my *Financial Test* chapter. This chapter allowed me to be authentic regarding the tough lessons I had to learn about my finances after experiencing a few bankruptcies. Though I was very disappointed in myself, I was able to rebuild from some of the lowest moments of my life. I decided to be open about my finances in this chapter because I know there are some individuals who have experienced similar struggles. If I can use my lessons to help just one person, I have accomplished what I need to.

In my *Family Test* chapter, I discuss the good, bad, complicated, difficult, sad, frustrating, proud and rewarding moments with my family. My big sister and I experienced many challenges as young girls living in our mother's household. I watched my sister get hit by a car while walking home from school. When she got hit, my mother ran to her to ensure she was not alone in the ambulance. It was such a scary time for us. My mother was not perfect, but she did what she could to keep us protected. My sister dealt with bullies at school. When a boy at school would not leave her alone, my mom slapped the boy, which resulted in her going to jail. My mother did not play about her girls! Though our actions have consequences, my sister never had to worry about the boy bothering her again. We also experienced an eviction growing up, which meant we had to live with my grandmother briefly before being highly encouraged to live with my father.

After moving in with my father, a lot changed. We spent a lot of time in church. We took family trips. We made a lot of memories at the family reunions we had over the years. Those memories encouraged my oldest brother to start the family reunions again. In July 2023, my father's side of the family hosted a family reunion for the first time in a while. When my brother was born, I lost my "baby" title. Though I was not happy losing my "baby" title, I was grateful for the close bond my baby brother and I developed over the years. In 2017, he made me an auntie to a baby boy. I was filled with so much joy. Every year, we travel to Nashville, Tennessee to celebrate his birthday. In 2020, in the midst of a pandemic and a limited guest list, I witnessed my brother get married. My baby brother evolved as a husband and father. Through the good and bad, family is everything. I have learned to cherish each moment while we can and that is conveyed in my *Family Test* chapter.

In *Relationship Test Part II,* I discuss the challenges my significant other, DE, and I endured as we attempted to cultivate a healthy and happy relationship, though circumstances worked against us. I share the good, bad and complicated moments we went through as a couple. *Did we really have the substance to stay together?* This chapter covers all the details regarding our current relationship status and more. It is labeled Part II because I included a *Relationship Test* chapter in my first book. Finally, "Resilience" concludes with the *Friend Test* chapter. This chapter introduces individuals who play a major role in my life, individuals who are like family, and individuals who I had to cut ties with. It is important to surround ourselves with people who pour into us as much as we pour into them. It is necessary to keep individuals close who reciprocate the same support and authenticity that is given. I am intentional about letting go and releasing individuals who no longer serve a purpose in my life. Though getting to this point in my life was hard, it was necessary for my growth.

"Resilience" takes readers on a journey of hope, healing, restoration and reflection. It is authentic, passionate and

iii

transparent. These experiences are real. It was past experiences that helped me grow into a better woman, mother, partner, friend, sister, auntie, daughter and coworker. I want to share with the world again that the past does not define me. The challenges I have endured in this life have equipped me for the future. If there is anyone dealing with home, finance, family, relationships, and/or friend tests, understand that, if I can get through it, so can you. If I can grow through it, so can you. Never give up. Those who are meant to be in your life will remain in your life. Those whose time in your life has expired, let them go. For the relationships Jesus has asked you to mend, do so before it is too late. Time is too precious to waste. Life is getting shorter. Remember, obedience is better than sacrifice. Do what Jesus has asked you to do. You are resilient!

CHAPTER 1: HOME TEST

Most individuals, young or old, desire a place they can call their own. It does not matter if it is a long-term renter or homeowner, we all desire our own space to call home. It is essential to have a safe haven. "Home is where the heart is" is true in most cases. This simply means, no matter what or where the place of residence is located, there is an emotional and sometimes a spiritual attachment that draws you to that space. When I began my stability journey in 2008, it included creating a safe space my son and I could call home. It was important for me to be close to work and in a suitable school district. It was necessary to be in an area where I felt safe as a single mom. Affordability was a major factor as well. When I decided to move into an apartment community in Mableton, Georgia, it was because it was affordable, convenient and quiet. The community was small, and I felt safe. It was truly a hidden blessing.

The apartment complex was not an upscale community with amenities, but it was a peaceful place I could call home. A few months after I moved in, a female tenant moved in next door. She became a sister-friend. We always looked out for one another. We had a lot in common, which meant we could relate to each other well. We were both single women with a child to raise. She had a daughter, and I had Alijah. Many days and nights we would stand outside on the balcony and talk to each other for hours. It was refreshing having someone to talk to and a person who did not mind listening, too. In addition to our long talks, she would invite

1

me over to her place to eat. She always shared her delicious meals with Alijah and me. Since Alijah was a latch-key kid, having a responsible adult next door looking out for us both made a huge difference. We took turns babysitting for one another, and if I needed something, she looked out for me. Of course, when she needed me, I was right there. I was extremely grateful for our friendship. She was truly my sister friend.

The leasing staff was a pleasure to deal with as well. Every individual I encountered was very professional and pleasant. I never had any major issues. When challenges did arise, as they sometimes did, they were resolved quickly. Even though the move-in process went well, I knew I wanted more. I realized apartment life was just not for me. It wasn't that I felt I was too good to live in an apartment, I was just not willing to accept others' behaviors and habits when they impacted my living situation. To my surprise, the neighbors downstairs - who had children - were not as clean as I expected them to be. When I would leave my home to head to work or to run errands, I would see food, drinks, cups and bottles outside on the ground. I could not understand why. *Who was dropping trash outside and not picking it up? Why were they being lazy? Was it the kids, adults or both? Was it that difficult to pick up something after it had fallen on the ground?* If the outside area was nasty, I could only imagine what the inside looked like. I could not understand why it was so hard for adults to be clean and organized.

In most cases, children do what they see. Therefore, if they see Mom and Dad leave trash around everywhere, they will do the same. This explained why I was dealing with a problem in my home,

2

and I was not happy. The way a person treats their home is not my business, that is, until it impacts my space. I took pride in keeping my home neat, clean and, clutter free. I am very minimalistic, so I never had a lot of stuff. After routine cleaning throughout the apartment every other day and keeping my kitchen spotless, I could not understand why I started seeing bugs. Yes, bugs. The brown bugs no one wants in their home. I was livid. I did not want to deal with brown bugs simply because my neighbors were not clean. I immediately called the leasing office to request pest control.

Thankfully, the weekly treatments helped, and the downstairs neighbors eventually moved. When things returned back to normal, I was relieved. After some time passed, I decided I did not want to move from my current apartment just to go to another apartment community. I wanted to stay put as long as possible, and when it was time to move, I wanted to move into a house. In 2015, after only a few months with my current employer, I was able to move into a house. Yes, I would still be renting, but I would no longer be in an apartment community. Since I had established an exceptional payment history and my credit was in good standing, it was a seamless process to obtain approval for a home. Still in Mableton, and less than a mile away from my apartment, I found a condominium with three bedrooms and three bathrooms for $900 a month. I contacted the realtor to schedule a tour. I was extremely impressed with the professionalism demonstrated by the realtor. She answered all my questions, providing details regarding the application process and deposit cost. She provided a realistic timeframe for when I could expect to receive a decision. Within about three days, she called to let me

3

know my application was approved. I was overly excited. Alijah and I would have a new place to call home after experiencing apartment life consistently for six years.

Since collaborating with realtors and renting homes was a familiar process, I was hopeful my new home would serve its purpose until I was ready to buy. After obtaining the approval for the new home and moving in, I experienced a major challenge. On day one, we did not have hot water. That meant I could not clean the way I needed to or take hot showers. *Why was this a problem?* I set up a new account with Georgia Power a week before moving in and made sure all utilities were set up under my name prior to moving in. When I called Georgia Power, the representative confirmed the service was on and that I should check to determine if the pilot was lit. She advised that there was nothing else she could do since the service was active and on. Even though I was working for a natural gas provider at the time, I was not familiar with lighting pilots. *What did that even mean?* My next option was to call the owner of the property. This was the first time I needed to call or talk to the owner about anything since the only person I communicated with during the application process was the realtor. Even though this was the first call to the owner, unfortunately it became the first of many. I was pretty upset about not having hot water, so I did not know what to expect when I contacted the owner. When I explained that there was no hot water in the home, he sounded concerned. The next day, he sent a contractor to check the hot water heater. The contractor determined the hot water heater needed to be replaced. When I shared that information with the owner, he was shocked. He could

4

not believe the water heater needed to be replaced. That was not my problem. All I knew was that my son and I needed hot water. We would not live in a home without hot water. That was not an option.

By the second day in our new home, we still did not have hot water. The owner was terribly slow in his efforts to resolve the issue. My patience ran thin. I was not happy. All I wanted to know was when my son and I would have hot water. As a new tenant, I expected the owner to have a sense of urgency, yet he lacked this quality. I quickly learned he was slow to resolve most issues at the property. The owner finally replaced the water heater after several days without hot water. I was thankful. Hot water, I realized, is just one of many things we take for granted until we do not have it. After the episode with the hot water, the chaos continued.

One morning as I backed out of my garage to head to work, I hit something. When I pulled forward back inside my garage, I got out of the car in a hurry to figure out what prevented me from getting out of my own garage. I assessed my car for damages. Thankfully there was no damage. I was grateful, but fuming. *How would I explain to the insurance company that I damaged my car while backing out of the garage?* It sounds so silly. I discovered the thing I backed into was another car. The anger and frustration I felt in that moment was indescribable. *What idiot parked their car in my driveway overnight? What made them feel that was appropriate to do? Who did not realize someone moved into this property months ago?* I got back in my car and blew the horn. Yes, I laid on the horn until I got tired of hearing it. I could tell my neighbors were trying to figure out what was going on because I

5

started seeing them look out their windows. That was the plan. To blow my horn until the owner of the car came out to move it from my driveway. After honking for 30 minutes, no one came. Since my shift started at 7 a.m., it was routine for me to leave home by 6 a.m. to allow time for traffic or any other delays. It was already 6:30 a.m., and I could not get out of my own driveway. *What was I supposed to do? "Should I call the police?"* I asked myself.

First, I had to call my job to tell them I would be late. I take pride in being on time, so being late to work due to someone else's negligence did not sit well with me. Second, after speaking to my manager at work, I realized I had to call the police. My job expected me to provide them with a copy of the incident report. A bit puzzled by the request, I was upset all over again. *Did they think I was lying? Did they think my request was bogus?* I guess it did sound pretty silly. *"I am very sorry. I am running late today because I cannot get out of my garage."* Yes it did sound silly, but that was my reality.

The more I thought about it, the more upset I became. The situation was truly baffling. It was quickly approaching 8 a.m., and I was still stuck in my garage. I finally called the police and impatiently waited for them to arrive. Upon arrival, I explained to the officer what happened. I attempted to leave my house for work and realized I was blocked by an unknown car in my driveway. The officer mentioned there was nothing they could do since the car was on private property. However, he did suggest having the car towed at my expense. The situation was unreal. I literally rolled my eyes thinking to myself, he cannot be serious. I asked the officer, *"Do you think it is fair for me to pay to have an unknown, unauthorized vehicle moved from a property I rent?"* I called the

6

property owner. He did not answer. That was typical for him. He never answered when I called. My anger escalated. Before I had a moment to verbalize my frustration, the officer offered to run the license plate. He mentioned that running the license plate would help determine who the car was registered to. I finally felt a sigh of relief. Within a few moments the officer walked over to me and advised that the car was a rental from Enterprise. After he provided me with all the information he found, he gave me a case number and left. I contacted the closest Enterprise location to my home. I was relieved it was the location the car had been rented from. A female representative answered the phone. She was very helpful, and I could tell she sensed my desperation. I told her if the renter of the car was not located soon, I would have the car towed.

After providing her with my address, she discovered the individual who rented the car lived in my neighborhood. I never doubted that. I just did not realize the individual was only three houses down. She contacted the driver on my behalf. Within a few short moments, a young male, who looked like he was in his early 20s, came rushing to my driveway. He was very apologetic. He looked scared. Maybe the representative from Enterprise provided him with all the details. Or, maybe it was the expression on my face. Without thinking I asked, "What made you park your car in someone else's driveway? Is this what everyone does in the neighborhood?" He responded, "I am so sorry. I did not realize someone lived here." I was very confused because by that time I had lived in the home for months. The fact that I parked my car in the driveway several times before moving it into the garage made it more puzzling. Impatiently, I asked him to move the car so I could

7

get to work. It was now three hours later from my initial attempt to leave for work. I was very frustrated when I finally made it to work. However, I had to put my personal challenges aside and do my job.

A few weeks after the rental car episode, I discovered my next door neighbor was a football parent who I knew from the park. Alijah played football for three years, sixth through eighth grade. Although the parent next door was not someone I knew on a personal level, I knew she was not the cleanest. I wondered if it could get any worse, and it did. One afternoon when I left home, there was a container of wings, celery and dressing in the middle of the street. The food was directly in front of both our homes. I was livid. *Is this really happening? Why would someone drop food in the street and not pick it up?* Eventually, I started noticing brown roaches in my kitchen. I was not happy. After day two of a slight invasion, I could not take it anymore. I called the property owner, but he did not answer. This was the second time he was unreachable.

Anxious to get the issue resolved, I texted him. I was very detailed in my message regarding the problem. After some time passed, he called me. I was surprised it took so long for him to call me back. At that moment, I wondered if I made the right decision moving to the property. The owner was very slow in communicating with me. At times, he was unresponsive. In addition, he seemed to make excuses about why he could not get to something immediately. It was very alarming. When I explained to him what was going on with the bug problem, his response was, "There has never been a bug problem in the home." I shared with him that while that was probably true when he occupied the property several years ago, there was obviously a problem now. To prevent a back and forth, I simply asked, "What are you going to do to resolve the problem?" When he responded with the same comment he made previously, I knew he had no intention of helping.

I was bothered, but I knew I had to find a solution quickly. Since there was a slight problem at the previous apartment I lived in, I contacted the leasing manager to get pest control details. The similar issue in my last apartment was quickly resolved, so I thought the leasing manager could help. I spoke with her briefly, and she provided me with the pest control company's name and number. After speaking with the owner of the business, he provided available dates and times he could stop by and assess the problem. Thankfully, he was able to treat the home the same day. Upon arrival, we recapped what I was experiencing and the best treatment method. He was concerned about the effectiveness of the treatments in my home since he could not treat the home next door too. The home next door was the reason for the problems in my home. I understood his concerns, but I wanted to take the chance to see if it would work. He was very professional, knowledgeable and thorough. He treated the inside and outside of the home. He suggested a monthly treatment plan to get started. I agreed and covered the cost out of my pocket. He was shocked that the owner of the property did not contribute to the pest control cost. I explained to him I would be reimbursed one way or another.

Once he completed all treatments, I reached out to the owner to let him know what was done. He did not have much to say. I explained I would wait for reimbursement or deduct the cost from my next rent payment. Several weeks passed and I still had not received a payment. Bothered by the owner's lack of communication and professionalism, I tried not to dwell on it much. When it was time to pay rent, I deducted the cost of pest control from the total and dropped off the difference. He gave no push back. If he had pushed back, I was ready to stand my ground because he was not doing right by me as a tenant. I contacted the pest control company after the first treatments were completed and told the owner the treatments really helped. Although the neighbors were still next door, my problem had been resolved. When they moved out, however, I experienced another problem.

Maintaining a home with filth and bad habits from others next door was very difficult. I came to the realization that living in a townhome was as bad as living in an apartment community. The way my neighbors lived impacted me. When the neighbors moved out, they left the place in a really bad state. It was nicknamed the "dumping ground" by the homeowner's association. It was bad. Trash, food, bags, debris, clothing and furniture were everywhere. *How could anyone live this way? How could a woman with kids live this way?* It was shocking. No matter what was happening next door, I had to protect my space. I scheduled pest control to return to the home and treat inside and out. When pest control treated outside, he confirmed just how bad things were next door. Extremely concerned the treatment would not work this time, I asked what I should do to ensure the treatment worked. He could not guarantee the treatments would work, but he was willing to offer discounted treatments if more were needed. I was truly

10

grateful for the gesture. Within about three weeks, my home was cleared of brown bugs. Ecstatic and relieved, I called the pest control company to share the good news. It was encouraging to walk in my kitchen, living room, and dining room without being greeted by unwelcome visitors. Even though I no longer had issues with bugs, I was still dealt with ongoing challenges inside the property. When I moved into the neighborhood in 2015, I was unaware of the various issues the homeowner's association dealt with.

Homeowners were not paying their HOA fees, which were supposed to be used to pay the water bill in the community. The Cobb County Water System threatened to turn off water in the entire community because the bill was so far behind. The HOA Board developed a water project that consisted of installing individual water meters on each home. That meant homeowners and/or renters would be responsible for covering the water bill. Initially, I approved of the upcoming changes. My son and I were not using a lot of water, so I figured the water bill would be very minimal. Then, I noticed the kitchen faucet dripped water consistently. It started all of a sudden. In addition to the kitchen faucet, the showerhead in the master bathroom dripped as well. The anxiety I felt at that moment built up. *What else would happen? Why was so much happening back-to-back? Is this what it feels like to own a home? Would I have the same problems as a homeowner?* I couldn't understand why I had to deal with so much. Talking to the owner of the property was pointless. He dragged his feet about every issue I shared. He had a nonchalant attitude, and I learned very quickly he was cheap. If it cost money, he was going to find the most inexpensive way to get it resolved. I was blown away by his lack of care for his property. If I owned property, whether it was an investment property or a home I lived in, I would take care of it to ensure the value would not depreciate. He did not think the way I did, and that alarmed me. Frankly, I cared more about his property than he did. My frustration grew. I went to Home Depot and bought a new faucet for the kitchen. I spent my own money, yet again, to resolve another issue. Thankfully, the HOA president was gracious enough to replace it for me without any additional cost. I did ask, however, what he would normally charge and included that cost for the property owner. His cost and the cost of supplies were more than $100. I shared that information with the owner. Once again, I had to deduct the cost from my rent payment. It was clear he had no intention of reimbursing me for the items I fixed in the home. I could not understand why he was not willing to support me in resolving these issues. It was overwhelming. One thing after the other. The goal was to ensure my bills were not higher than usual due to water leaks in the home.

Soon after the issue in the kitchen was resolved, I was, yet again, tasked with fixing another issue - the dripping shower head in the master bedroom. I knew reaching out to the property owner would be a waste of time, so I did not bother. After reaching out to multiple plumbers and describing the issue, a plumber from Roto Rooter came to assist. When the plumber arrived, he told me what needed to be done. I signed off on the work order. Three hours and $350 later, the leak was resolved. I was relieved, but disappointed I had to cover the cost of the repairs from my pocket. I reached out to the property owner to let him know the water leaks were resolved. I expressed to him that I was expecting reimbursement since I covered the cost for issues in the home that were his responsibility to cover. Since he had not reimbursed me for previous repairs in the home, I knew this time would be no different.

After two months of paying my rent in full with no reimbursement, I finally deducted $350 from my rent payment. In addition, I made a copy of the receipt which supported the cost and included it in an envelope with my rent payment. I was exhausted and concerned. I tried to wrap my head around the fact that in such a short time, I had covered the cost of numerous repairs, pest control, and supplies to ensure I was not impacted negatively by the growing problems. I just did not understand why the care for my well-being was very minimal. It was upsetting. I decided to add renter's insurance to my monthly expenses. For bundling my car insurance with renter's insurance, I received a discount from Progressive. While I kept renter's insurance when I lived in the apartment complex, I never had to file a claim. I figured renters insurance was vital for the new property because there were several things going wrong.

After the issues were resolved in the kitchen and master bathroom, I thought things would be better. For a very short time, things did go well. I had no further issues with bugs or running water. However, other problems developed. It rained pretty badly one day when I got home. I was grateful when I finally pulled into the garage and walked into the house. The only advantage of living at the property was that it had a garage which, meant I did not get wet when it rained. Due to the issues from next door, I never kept

13

garbage in the house. Typically, I placed everything in a plastic bag and walked it outside to the dumpster. The dumpster was conveniently located outside my back door to the right of the fence.

As I proceeded out the back door to take out the trash, I walked across a small, yet growing puddle of water on the carpet. My mood changed immediately from calm and peaceful to disgust. *What now? Was every single thing in the house broken? Why was there always something going wrong at this property?* My blood was boiling with rage. My heart was racing. My head was pounding. My hands were shaking. At that moment, I realized living at the property was starting to take a toll on my well-being. I was not happy. It was time to make some changes ASAP. I had to make that dreaded call to the property owner again. He never answered my call. I was extremely disappointed, but not surprised. I would finally receive communication from him only after I sent a text message. That was also frustrating. None of it made sense, and I refused to dwell on it. I made my complaint very quickly, "Water is coming from outside onto the carpet when it rains. *What are you going to do, and when are you going to do it?*" I made it clear to him I could not resolve the problem. I was not going to resolve the problem. I made sure the back door was shut tight and locked to prevent more water from coming in. The property owner told me he would stop by to check on the problem. My anger intensified due to his lack of urgency. Before I realized it, I asked him again, "*When are you coming? Are you bringing an experienced professional with you? How quickly will you get this resolved?*" He assured me he would arrive within the next 24 hours.

14

When he arrived the next day, he had a lot of questions for me as I figured he would. There was one question that really rubbed me the wrong way. "Are you closing the back door completely?" He asked. Before I could think about my response, I asked, *"Does the door look secure to you? Or does it look open?"* I reassured him I was not the problem. It was his responsibility to resolve all issues occurring on his property. To keep my emotions in check, I walked upstairs to my bedroom. I felt like the property owner purposely said things to get under my skin, but I was not going to allow him to steal my joy. After an hour of assessing the issue, he still did not know what caused the water to come inside the home. For a while, I only noticed water on the carpet when it rained. When the sun was out, there were no water puddles on the carpet.

The issue was ongoing. The off and on water coming in through the back door was causing damage to the carpet. I noticed that Alijah kept blowing his nose, sneezing, and even wheezing. I tried to figure out what was going on. *Why was my son wheezing?* He had asthma as a small child but there had not been any instances of wheezing in many years. After wrestling with myself for some time, I came to the realization our home was potentially impacted by mold. If it was mold, what were we supposed to do? We could not live in a home where mold was a problem. *Where would we go?* I was officially concerned my son and I were inhaling mold. The next day, I told the property owner I was filing a claim with my renters insurance company for temporary housing. I made it clear that if I had to secure temporary housing, I would once again reduce my rent payment for each day I could not stay in the home.

15

I was tired of needing to take such drastic measures to ensure my son and I were safe and protected. It was draining. *When would the nightmare end?* I had endured so much in the first year living on the property that I was becoming numb. The property owner had an inability to resolve issues timely or effectively. He lacked communication skills. He lacked empathy. He showed no care or concern for us. I was blown away. Later that evening, he came over to inspect the carpet. He finally discovered the water was coming inside from the unit next door.

Since the unit was vacant, he turned the water off in hopes of resolving the problem. Then he pulled up the carpet by the back door. The water damage was clearly visible. He assured me there would be someone there within the next few days to replace the carpet. For the first time since moving into the property, he kept his word. When I got home from work the next day, the entire downstairs area had new carpet. I was glad the water issue was finally resolved. Unfortunately, the issues continued. I knew it was time to explore other housing options fast. My son was in his last year of high school, and I did not want to enroll him in a new school for one year. I just did not feel that was a good decision. Therefore, I wanted to make sure wherever we moved, it was still in the same area.

There were not many homes in the area to choose from. Since signing my first lease in 2015, I refused to sign a new one. There were just too many issues to even consider signing a new lease. Typically, when a new lease is not signed, landlords, property management companies, or leasing staff can increase the rent to market rates. Due to the ongoing challenges I faced, I was prepared

16

to give the property owner a piece of my mind if he increased the rent. The increase did not come immediately, but it did come. Supposedly, the property owner was receiving a lot of backlash from the HOA about not having an active lease on file for all tenants. I understood their guidelines. However, the owner never seemed to follow the rules. After going back and forth with the property owner and letting him know he was wrong and unprofessional, we mutually agreed to a $75 rent increase. I moved into the property in January 2015. It was now the end of 2018, and I just signed a new lease. In February 2019, I received word from the HOA that the property owner could no longer rent out his properties in the community because he failed to complete necessary paperwork by the deadline. I was not surprised. It seemed the property owner had an inability to do anything right. I found out his other tenant had already moved out. The HOA made it clear that he had to move back into the home or sell it. He could no longer rent. I was very concerned. Although the living experience had not been great, I was not ready to move. The packing, unpacking, cleaning, organizing, planning and preparing was too overwhelming.

I reached out to the HOA president to determine any possible options. I explained my concerns and asked if I could have more time to find a new place. The HOA president was very understanding and approved a one-year extension. Relieved and grateful, I reassured him I would work timely to find a new place. I communicated the news to the property owner. He was impressed. He wanted to know what I said or did to get an extension. There is a thing called "favor" that is not always fair. Since the favor of God

17

is all over my life and he was already working things out for me in the background, I did not share any details regarding the extension. The specific details were not important. Unfortunately, the one-year extension came and went quickly. The property management company was still very adamant about not allowing the property owner to rent it out. Considering he had not been the greatest landlord, I understood the need to get rid of him.

I started looking for a new home to rent. When I found possible options, I started completing applications. Sadly, due to credit challenges back then, I kept getting denied. My anxiety grew. The worry I felt intensified. What was I going to do? I had officially received written notification that I had 90 days to vacate. If I did not vacate in 90 days, the property owner would be charged $100 per day, for each day he leased to me without proper authorization. I emailed the HOA president once again to explore any additional options. Due to the pandemic in 2020 and constant denials, I was granted a final extension. When I communicated this information back to the property owner, he pushed back. He indicated he did not approve of another extension and expected me to vacate the home at the end of the 90-day period.

I was livid. *Was he serious? Why was he acting like a jerk?* Though I was not surprised by his behavior, I was highly disappointed. I reminded him we were in the middle of a pandemic, and I simply needed more time. After a lot of back and forth, he finally agreed to let me stay until Dec. 31, 2020. He made it clear there would be no more extensions. In addition, I received another rent increase. Extremely annoyed, I accepted the increase and started planning to move as soon as possible. It was April 2020 and

I had eight months remaining to find a place to live. I did not have a problem finding a home. My issue came with obtaining an approval. When I found a home, I applied. In the end, I was either instantly denied, or I never heard back.

At that point, I had not considered going back to an apartment complex. Even though I had such a terrible experience with the current property owner, I valued the extra space. I enjoyed having two levels. I loved having a garage to park my car in. I appreciated being close to Alijah's school. The area was peaceful and quiet. However, I knew I had to find something sooner than later.

One of my high school classmates who I considered a friend was my go-to for everything real estate. I never thought she would be able to help with rental properties, but it was worth a try. After receiving several denials, I reached out to her to get feedback, suggestions, or any tips that would help my moving process. I was very transparent. I let her know I had to move soon but kept receiving unfavorable results. We talked at length regarding my unique situation. In the end, she did not have any resources to share with me right away. She assured me if she heard of or found anything she would let me know. For that, I was grateful.

A few weeks later, my friend reached out to me. By that time, it was July 2020. I had just purchased a new car. My finances were in order and I was officially ready to change my living space. Though I still had five months left, I was desperately ready to move. My realtor friend had a client who was closing on a new home and was interested in renting out his current home. I was hopeful. She gave me all the details regarding location, size and availability. The

19

size of the home was the exact size I was currently living in - three bedrooms, three bathrooms, and two levels. The only downside was the property was no longer in Cobb County, and it did not have a garage. Not being in Cobb County anymore was fine. I knew I would be back if it was God's will. No longer having a garage was a tough blow since I had just purchased a new car. However, she told me the community was gated which was a major plus for me. She sent me a video of the property, and I was very impressed. She told me she would set up a meeting with the owner if I was interested.

I was extremely interested in that property. I needed a fresh start more than ever. She coordinated a date and time to meet the owner. One Sunday morning before heading to church, Alijah and I stopped by. The video did not do the home any justice. It was beautiful. The owner seemed to take pride in his home. It was clean, organized, decorated well, and smelled good. Not to mention the owner made recent upgrades to the countertops and island in the kitchen. At the end of the tour, both the property owner and realtor asked, "What do you want to pay for rent?" Shocked and stunned, it took me a moment to gather my words. I was truly speechless. After a few seconds, I looked at the owner and my realtor friend and asked, "Is this a serious question?" They both said yes at the same time. Wow, I thought. They were being more than lenient by asking me what I wanted to pay for rent. I needed a few seconds to think, but I finally gave them an amount. The owner accepted. Feeling overwhelmed with gratitude was an understatement. I was elated! The owner said because I came highly recommended, there would be no credit or background check. All I had to do was pay rent and the deposit. In addition, I

20

was given the opportunity to pay the security deposit in three installments. I was grateful. I always believe God will truly make a way even when we cannot see a way. I was very excited about moving. I sent a message to my landlord to inform him I would be moving out of the property by the end of August.

For the first time since I moved in, the property owner seemed disappointed. I did not care. I was overjoyed that my time in his property was coming to an end. Unfortunately, the new owner experienced a delay in closing. Therefore, I was not able to move out of the current home before the first of September as anticipated. My move-in date was delayed until September 10th. That meant I would still owe the current owner rent for at least 10 days. Considering the owner was holding a security deposit totaling $900, it made sense to me to deduct the 10 days of rent from that balance. He felt differently. Once again, he made things complicated. The way he thought about and handled things bothered me a lot.

To go along with the craziness, I agreed to pay rent and release the keys at the same time. I moved everything out of the home. I cleaned the home from top to bottom. As agreed, I dropped off the rent check, garage opener, and keys. I blocked and deleted him from both mobile devices so he could not contact me again. Then I contacted my bank and placed a stop payment on the rent check. It did not make sense for him to require me to pay anything given my experience and the fact that he owed me a refund from my security deposit. I did not dwell on it. I was glad to no longer live on his property. I prayed the new home would be a

21

much better experience. I released all the previous negative energy. I was adamant about a fresh start.

My move-in day was extremely busy. From last minute cleaning, packing, throwing things out I no longer needed, to making minor repairs, there was a lot going on at once. Not to mention my movers were running late. Apparently, their truck broke down, and dispatch had to assist with getting them back on the road. I was puzzled that no one bothered to call me to let me know what was going on. My movers were scheduled to arrive at 10 a.m. By 10:15 a.m., I was calling dispatch to determine if they were still coming. The courtesy of letting me know what happened instead of needing to call the company would have been ideal. As I get older, I realize I cannot expect others to conduct business the way I do.

The movers finally arrived about an hour later than scheduled. I knew the delay would cause some major challenges for me as I was preparing to travel for my baby brother's wedding the very next day. I had hair and makeup scheduled. In addition, I had more errands to run before I left Atlanta. The day was becoming very hectic. Thankfully, I got rid of a lot of old furniture and things I no longer needed. Since I got rid of a lot of big furniture, there was not much that had to be moved. Besides my son's bed and living room furniture, I only had boxes. The movers were efficient and loaded the truck timely. I completed one final walk through and my time at the old home was over. I was hopeful for the new beginning. Although I was moving out of Cobb County, I was only about six minutes away. My new home was very close and for that I was grateful.

22

We left Cobb County for the first time in 15 years. It was bittersweet. When we arrived at our new space, the movers went back to work and moved everything in. It took a little time to unload things because there was carpet on the second level. Due to the light color of the carpet, I did not allow shoes upstairs at all. I knew immediately when I completed my walk through that no shoes would be allowed. I wanted to preserve the carpet as much as possible. I was intentional about treating homes as if it were my own. Many of the movers had shoe covers, so they used those to take furniture upstairs. For the other movers who did not have shoe covers, they had to leave their shoes at the door. Once everything was unloaded and accounted for, the movers went on their way.

The property owner came by shortly after. He wanted to make sure I did not have any issues getting in or accessing doors. Having the owner of the property live in the same neighborhood was convenient. It meant if anything was needed, he was just a short walk or drive away. While he was there, I asked, *"How soon are you looking to sell this home?"* His response was, *"I am willing to rent as long as you need to be here."* I was truly relieved. I did not want to move again until I was able to buy a home which would be in two years. Since he mentioned verbally that he was willing to rent to me for two years and the lease had just started, I did not think it was necessary to put anything in writing. However, I quickly learned getting things in writing was vital. We were still amid a global pandemic, and there were several individuals who were struggling to make rent payments. By God's grace, I was able to make my payments before they were due. Most months I made my

23

rent payments by the 25th. This was the first time I was able to pay before time or by the 1st every single month. Not to mention the payments for that property was higher than I ever paid for rent. I was blessed beyond words. The first six months went by quickly.

Between traveling, working, tutoring, writing my first book, and spending time with family and friends, time seemed to be moving quickly. The property owner and I had no major issues. If something was going on at the property, he worked to resolve things right away. He made a conscious effort to timely handle any issues that arose. Sometimes I did have to wait. I experienced challenges with the heat not working, a leak in my son's bathroom, a busted water heater and a spider problem. In addition, there was once a plumbing issue. Of course, the property owner wanted to know what I was doing differently in the home since he never experienced these challenges. I reassured him I was not doing anything wrong. Things do happen and things did happen. In May 2021, I revisited the conversation about renting another year. Once again, the property owner verbally confirmed renting another year would be fine. Since the realtor friend assisted me with the current property, I was confident I would remain informed regarding any decisions concerning the home. I was so wrong.

I signed my lease in September 2020 with an end date of Aug. 31, 2021. On Aug. 2, 2021, after almost a year of not hearing anything from the realtor classmate, I received a text asking if I could talk. I felt in my spirit something was not right. I knew something was wrong. I informed her I was headed to lunch within a few minutes and would give her a call. As the clock wined down for lunch, the knots in my stomach intensified. Anxiety built. *What*

24

did she need to discuss? Why was I hearing from her now after all this time? What had she discussed with the property owner? What were they both plotting, and why now? Well, I received all the answers to my questions and more. When my lunch officially started, I picked up my phone and dialed her number. After unnecessary small talk, she informed me the property owner was ready to sell the home. I was disgusted. My blood boiled. I asked, *"Are you kidding me? When did he make that decision, and why now?"* I was upset. Not because the owner went against what he verbally told me, but because he waited until the last minute to mention it. Truth was, he did not tell me. He was being a coward. He had the realtor do his dirty work. The unfortunate reality was she willingly obliged his antics. It was now less than 30 days before my lease expired, and I was informed I had to move. I was livid. I was boiling with rage. I was baffled by the property owner's total disregard for the verbal conversation we had just three months prior. I understand things change, but communication is key. There is no reason why the property owner should have waited until the lease was almost over to disclose this information. Not to mention he never told me his intentions.

The realtor was officially doing all the work. He left the planning and communication to her. She was so involved with the process and leading the efforts that I asked her if I needed to start sending the rent payments to her. She confirmed all payments should still be sent to the property owner, even though he was no longer communicating with me. It was unbelievable. Soon I learned the realtor was more concerned about the commission profit than about whether my son and I would have a place to lay our heads.

25

Unfortunately, I was still learning tough lessons when it came to people and their true intentions. When people show you who they are, it is vital to believe them.

For a while I felt the property owner and realtor had my best interest at heart. However, I was wrong. The property owner stopped answering my calls. He would not respond to any messages sent via text. One of the last messages he sent to me was, "If you have any questions regarding the sale of the property, the realtor is the point of contact." I was blown away. Honestly, I was in disbelief. I could not understand why I was being treated this way. I was never late with rent payments. I never used a personal check to make rent payments. I used guaranteed funds and always paid before rent was due. I never had an eviction filed against me, and I treated the home as if it was my own since moving in September 2020. I learned quickly it was all about the money from both parties. It was currently a seller's market, and homes were selling for much more than they were worth a year prior. I was disappointed but not surprised by the lack of concern for my son and me. We were on the verge of being displaced. Prior to Aug. 3, 2021, no one reached out to me about needing to move. Again, the courtesy of letting me know what was going on would have been ideal. I immediately went into panic mode. *What was I going to do? Where was I going to go?* The realtor knew my struggle on a personal level, so it was baffling that I had to deal with this.

The next few days were extremely hectic. I agreed to allow a photographer to come take pictures of the home. Yes, they were already preparing to list the home and needed updated images. The purpose of the images was to prevent strangers from coming in and out of the home while we were still living there in the middle of a pandemic. Yes, the photographer took pictures of the home with my furniture, decorations, appliances, etc. I was puzzled, but pushed through, nonetheless. A few days later the home was officially on the market. The realtor made it seem as if she was looking out for me, but it was clear she was not. She was not obligated to do so. She was hired to do a job which was to sell the home.

I was granted a 60-day extension on the current lease. I felt it was the legal thing to do considering they did not provide proper notice. I was still very upset. I moved forward knowing I had to do what I had to do. Therefore, I started applying for more rental homes because I was still not able to buy. After numerous days of searching, I found a few affordable properties. However, the guidelines were strict and required a co-signer. Since I did not have a co-signer, the potential property was no longer an option. In the midst of trying to obtain a new home, the realtor informed me I had to allow in-person tours of the home. I was furious. *What was the purpose of having a photographer come take pictures if in the end in-person tours were still needed?* I was over it. Supposedly, the realtor could not get any potential buyers to commit to the deal without seeing the property first. Though I understood from a buyer's perspective, that was not my problem. The realtor convinced me that if I allowed in-person tours, it would potentially attract an investor who would want to keep the tenant in the home. I determined that was a lie. Everyone who was interested in the home wanted to occupy it. I was overwhelmed. My son and I were less than 60 days away from being displaced. I could not obtain approval for a new home or apartment. In addition, now I had to allow strangers in a home I was occupying. This situation bothered me a lot. Nevertheless, there was nothing I could do about it.

Potential buyers came and went. There were two to three tours per day. Individuals were late and did not follow my no-shoes-upstairs rule. I blamed the realtor because she should have communicated all these things before she scheduled tours. I finally made the decision to cease all in-person tours until I moved out of the property. The realtor was upset, but I did not care. I worked very hard to find a suitable place for my son and me to live but it was a challenge. From denials to being too expensive to afford, I was worried. At the beginning of October, I contacted Crestmark Apartment in Lithia Springs, Georgia. The leasing consultant was very informative and professional. I felt hopeful. After a lengthy conversation, I decided to schedule a tour.

The model apartments are always impressive, so it created false expectations of what the actual apartment would look like. Potential tenants could only view the models because there were no units available. I was hesitant, but I decided to apply. The rent was much higher than I was currently paying, but I knew God would help me through it. After I submitted my application, I waited. Shortly after, I received a call from the leasing office advising I was not approved with them directly, but I could apply through their partner option, Liberty Rent. Liberty Rent allows an approval option based on paying an access fee. The access fee equaled one month's rent and was non-refundable. I had so many questions. *What would happen if I paid another application fee and did not obtain an approval? Why is the access fee so much? Was this the best option?* My head was officially pounding. The anxiety was getting the best of me. *What should I do? Should I apply somewhere else or take my chances with Liberty Rent?* If I did not know anything else, I knew time was running out, and I needed a place for my son and me to live. After pondering back and forth, I decided to apply. The amount of money I spent on application fees was substantial. Eventually, I received instant approval. I was ecstatic! I was overjoyed! I was also very overwhelmed. If I could receive instant approval with Liberty Rent, why was I denied with everyone else? I did not have time to think too much about it.

I moved forward relieved that someone had finally approved me. I went back to work again, cleaning, organizing, purchasing moving supplies, hiring movers, and setting up utilities. I hate moving. There is always so much work involved. Here I was moving again after only 13 months. I was not happy, but I did what was necessary. The anger I felt toward the property owner and realtor grew. I still could not understand how they could be so inconsiderate for 1. waiting until the last minute to tell me I had to move 2. going back on the verbal agreement I thought was concrete 3. being so money-focused and insensitive about the entire situation. They were wrong, and Karma is real. I know God will pay every man according to his works, so I moved forward from that point encouraged.

On Oct. 15, 2021, I officially signed my lease with Crestmark. On Oct. 17, 2021, I moved completely out of the property in Atlanta. A few days later, the property owner texted me asking if I could allow a contractor access to check the roof. Initially, I wanted to completely ignore the message. Considering this was the same person who told me to contact the realtor if I had any questions about the sale of the property, how dare he ask me for anything? I quickly responded, *"No, I cannot. I have things to do."* Yes, I had completely moved out of the home, but had not told anyone or released the keys. Since I paid rent for the entire month of October and moved out on the 17th, a refund was due. I was doing what I wanted to do because I could. Within a few hours, I received a text from the realtor. She wanted to let me know she knew I moved out of the property. She even texted and congratulated me on finding a new place. I shut down that gesture very quickly. It lacked authenticity and I knew better. She was not the least bit concerned about me. Therefore, I handled her differently. She reached out to determine when a walk-through could be scheduled so the keys could be released. My response was, "These things will be done on my terms and will be communicated when I am ready." When the property owner went to the home to let the contractor in, he discovered I was gone because the home was completely empty. Again, I had not communicated with anyone because I was not ready. I was still pretty upset with them, so I minimized my communication until I was ready. Within a few days, I communicated a date and time to complete the walk-through. Supposedly, something came up and the realtor could no longer be present. That meant it would be just the property owner and me.

Still extremely upset, I was ready to get the walk through done. When I arrived at the home, I walked through one last time. Everything was spotless. I was standing in the living room talking on the phone when he arrived. Instead of entering the property, he

30

stood there and knocked on the door. I was so annoyed. *Why would an individual who owns a property knock on the door?* I was so confused. I asked, *"Why are you knocking on a door you own?"* It made no sense. I shook my head and continued my phone call. He checked everything on the main level before heading upstairs.

After a few moments, he met me back downstairs in the living room. He said everything looked good, so I immediately asked for my deposit. I paid my rent via Cash App. The property owner always received rent payments before it was due. I did not care what the normal process was, I was not willing to wait for a check to be mailed to me. I made that clear to him and the realtor. I informed him that I would not release the keys to the property until I received my deposit. I was unwavering in that decision. My response obviously took him by surprise because he was speechless. The realtor tried to call me, but I declined her call. I had nothing to say to her. As I mentioned before, things were now on my terms. I left the property and headed home. I emphasized to the property owner that I would release the keys when he had my deposit and not beforehand. A few days later I met him at the bank. He provided me with a cashier's check, and I provided him with all the keys to the property. I never communicated with either one of them again.

As I attempted to adjust to living in another new place, I decided to let go of the anger I felt. Learning about the greed of others caused me to part ways with an individual who I truly thought had my best interest at heart. It made me realize that in most cases it is about the money. We live in such a money-hungry world that things of this nature no longer surprise me. I know we

31

all must eat, but there are ways to handle situations the right way, without hurting others. When I moved out of Lithia Springs in 2007, I vowed to never go back. We should be careful when we use the word "never." God has a way of doing things opposite of what we think or intend.

When I arrived at Crestmark Apartments in Lithia Springs to sign my lease and pay the fees, I had not viewed my apartment. I communicated with the leasing staff that I would not be able to sign the lease or pay fees for a unit I had yet to see. Everyone understood my concerns. The leasing consultant and manager finally took me to see my unit. The manager warned me there were certain things she did not like and would work to get resolved. That made me very concerned. When I walked in, I was extremely disappointed. The drywall in the living room was damaged. It was a huge eye sore. I did not have the washer and dryer I was promised. My second bathroom had a cracked mirror. My closet shelves were old and dirty.

Later, I discovered my sockets did not work in the main bedroom. My water would not heat up. Not to mention, my front door had been kicked in. The door frame barely held on. There were so many things running through my head in that moment. *Was I in danger? Will the person responsible for kicking in the door come back again? What would the leasing office do to ensure my safety? Lastly, why was the apartment classified as move-in ready but in such bad shape?* I was mentally tired. The problems from the initial walk through were just the beginning. Returning to an apartment community for the first time since 2015 was frustrating as well. Previously when I lived in an apartment, I was on the top level. That was not the case at Crestmark. I was on the second level, and there were three floors in each building. It was a complete nightmare. There was stomping and bumping all day, every day. It never seemed to end. Since I am such a light sleeper, I hear every single noise. I was miserable. I signed a nine-month lease, and on day one I was ready to go. The luxury-style apartment community they portrayed online was not accurate.

The building overall was quiet. The neighbors' upstairs, who I quickly found out had three kids, were terrible. It blew my mind that the leasing office would assign me to that unit. I did not want to complain because I was happy to have been approved, however, the thought of my peace being disturbed was unsettling. When my washer and dryer were finally delivered, they left them sitting in my dining room instead of placing them in the laundry room. The maintenance team worked to resolve some issues while discovering others. I will say, the best part about my new living space was that I had a washer and dryer, which meant I did not have to pay to do laundry or commute to my parents' house. That was truly a blessing.

It was incredibly quiet when the neighbors above me were asleep or gone. After three short months, I was already over my new living space. It was a lot dealing with stomping and bumping all day, every day. I experienced so many bad sleepless nights. Thankfully, I had a second bedroom I could sleep in. No one should have to deal with this. I was desperately trying to restore my peace from the previous home, but I was fighting yet another battle. I strongly believe home is where I should find peace, comfort and safety. However, I found myself running into problems at each

33

place I moved into. When I shared my experiences with others, they often asked, *"Have you tried talking to your neighbors?"* My response was always no. Besides the constant complaints I made to the leasing office, I never said one word to any of my neighbors.

I was mentally tired. I was tired of moving, I was tired of renting. I was tired of the constant issues with property owners, realtors, and inconsiderate neighbors. I was tired of the enemy disturbing my peace. This was another home where I paid the rent before it was due. There was always a credit balance on my account. There were no delinquent payments, no eviction filings, and no lease violations. Yet, I experienced the worst living experience in Crestmark. The sad truth was my neighbors were not the only problem. It was the condition the unit was in when I arrived on day one. In addition, I experienced several water leaks from upstairs which started in the second bathroom. The leaks moved from the second bathroom to the living room. It was a lot. It was one thing after the other.

The maintenance team was in and out of my apartment every other day for one issue or another. There were new appliances in the apartment, but I was dealing with a leak coming from the refrigerator. The maintenance supervisor connected the icemaker which caused a refrigerator leak. Instead of sending the supervisor back to resolve the issue, the leasing office sent two associates who I realized were quite inexperienced. One accused me of installing the refrigerator incorrectly. I was blown away by the silly accusations. *How could I install the refrigerator incorrectly?* I was not the person responsible for installing the appliance in the apartment. It was there the same day I moved in. I was terribly upset. Soon after, I asked them to leave. I requested the leasing office to send the maintenance supervisor.

For the next few months, I avoided issuing any service requests. Then I realized there were still outstanding issues that had not been resolved. I created a list of all the things the leasing office promised they would complete at move-in, but had not handled. There was no logical explanation why things were not resolved. One afternoon while I was working from home, there was a knock on the door. I wondered who was knocking on my door in the middle of the day. When I opened the door, it was an unfamiliar individual. He mentioned he was there to help the property catch up on service requests since they were behind. It all made sense. Instead of communicating they were behind and bringing in additional support from the corporate office, the leasing staff never mentioned it. I was ready to go. My rent was close to $1,800 for a two-bedroom, two-bathroom apartment. How could I save for a home while paying out this kind of money every month for just rent? Not to mention, the apartment was not worth $1,800. I desperately needed change. In May 2022, there were exactly 60 days remaining before my lease ended. If I planned to vacate the apartment, I was required to submit a 60-day notice. If the notice was submitted in less than 60 days, I would be subject to damages. If I submitted the notice and changed my mind, I would be subject to damages which would be $250. It was insane.

I submitted my intent to vacate notice with the faith that God would see me through and bless me with a more affordable home. Looking and applying for homes was truly stressful. Rental properties were doubled what they were in 2021. Apartments were now more expensive to rent than rental homes. Single-family homes and condos had limited availability. Briefly, I considered staying where I was and renewing my lease. Then I received a renewal proposal for almost $1,900, and I knew it was time to go. There was no way I was going to pay $1,900 for a two-bedroom, two-bathroom apartment with serious issues. It was an unreal request, and I was just not willing to do it. I would not be able to adequately save for a home paying out that kind of money for rent. If $1,900 included all my monthly expenses it would be different, but it did not include everything.

I sat down and thought hard. *What am I going to do? Where was I going to go now?* Then I remembered my old apartment community in Mableton. It was a much smaller and older community, but suitable until I purchased my home. Since the community was small, the occupancy was always 100 percent. When I left the community in 2015, the property manager took pride in ensuring every unit was occupied. She was extremely sweet, professional, understanding and patient. People moved in and did not want to leave. I figured that had not changed. I decided to give her a call to inquire about vacancies. No matter how much time had passed since we last talked, she always remembered who I was. It was refreshing and encouraging. I discovered that for the first time in a long time the community had vacancies. I was profoundly grateful. God's timing is always perfect. The community only had one-bedroom apartments available. Even though this meant I would have to downsize again, I was willing to do whatever was necessary to secure a more affordable home. After speaking with the leasing manager for quite some time, I had all the information I needed to apply. She was 100 percent by the books and unwavering in that. I genuinely appreciated her for her efforts.

Later that same day, I applied for an apartment and paid the necessary fees. I was confident I would have favorable results because she provided all the requirements I needed to obtain approval. I needed at least a 600-credit score. My scores were beyond that. However, when she obtained my score, it reflected less than the requirement, which meant I was not automatically approved. Devastated, I asked her what I could do to obtain approval. The most important thing was proving that my credit scores were beyond the requirement. Unfortunately, there was nothing I could do to prove my scores were higher, but she did not give up.

She asked me to fill out a form for income and rental history verification. I completed this information and sent it back to her. She sent it to her manager to review. She asked if I could pay a security deposit equal to one month's rent. I quickly responded, *"Absolutely."* Within a few short days, I received the approval with one month's rent as my security deposit. I was truly relieved. I was grateful. I was ready to move. It was May, and in July I would be moving back to a community that was familiar and felt like home. My lease was set to expire July 13, 2022. A few weeks later, I received a call from the leasing manager from my new community. She shared with me that she had sad news. Being worried was an understatement. I wondered what she was preparing to tell me. I was concerned. The tenant who put in her letter of intent to vacate was no longer moving due to the sudden passing of her husband. I was heartbroken.

37

I extended my sincere thoughts and prayers to the tenant. I understood why she had to rescind her notice to vacate. She had nowhere else to go. *What would this mean for me? What was I going to do? Where was I going to go?* My mind was racing. I was afraid of what she would say next. The leasing manager shared with me that she could put me in one of the new apartments being built in the "E" building, but the rent would be more. I was elated. It did not matter where the apartment was or the increase in price, I would take it. I was no longer waiting for someone to move out but waiting for the contractors to finish the building. At the end of June, I reached out to my current apartment community to determine what my prorated rent would be. It was officially confirmed that I could move into my new place on July 20, 2022. The contractors were projected to complete everything by July 15. The prorated rent had not been updated to my online account. It only reflected rent for the first 13 days of July.

At the beginning of July, I went into the office to determine why there was a delay in updating my totals so I could pay rent. No one seemed to know why my balance had not been updated. I thought to myself, *"Lord, please get me out of here."* I was officially done. On July 3, I submitted my rent payment for the amount listed on my online profile. It was never updated to reflect 20 days vs. 13 days. To avoid late fees, I paid the amount listed for me to pay. From July 3-10, I checked my account to determine if any other fees were added. I still had a zero balance.

As I prepared to move again, I went to the store to get more boxes and moving supplies. I started packing in May and was ready to go. I had only a few things left to pack. Several days passed and there was no stomping or bumping coming from my neighbors upstairs. I was surprised but relieved. The same day, I discovered the neighbors from upstairs moved to another building. The timing was off. I was preparing to leave, too, so it did not matter if they were still above me or not. The peace was short-lived. As fast as the contractors and maintenance team made the unit move-in ready, a new tenant moved in. I asked God again to get me out of there. The week I was originally supposed to move, I learned the building had not been inspected, which meant we could not move in. There were still minor issues the company had to resolve before the certificate of occupancy could be issued. The situation was becoming overwhelmingly stressful. The saying is true in most cases, "What doesn't kill you, makes you stronger." However, the ongoing challenges with moving, obtaining approval, being denied, unprofessional leasing associates, and money-hungry realtors and property owners were becoming a little more than I wanted to deal with.

I went back to my current apartment community to determine if I could get more time. They told me no since my unit had already been pre-leased. *What was I going to do now? Where was I going to go until my apartment was ready?* I had movers scheduled to arrive the next day and I did not have a place for them to move my things to. I started panicking. I texted one of my sista friends and told her what was going on. I explained to her what I was dealing with because she dealt with something similar when she was preparing to close on her home. She was very empathetic and understanding. It was encouraging to have a circle of sisters who generated positive energy all the time.

39

Before we got off the phone, she offered to let me come to her house while I waited for my apartment to get ready. I was filled with pure joy. Until that moment, I had no idea where I was going, but God. He always, always, always, makes a way when we cannot see a way. He is faithful through it all. The next day was moving day. I picked up Alijah from my play sister's house. He was living with her so he could get back and forth to work. There were no buses in Lithia Springs so it made sense for him to stay with her. On moving day, he was such a tremendous help. I do not know what I would have done without him. He assisted with the entire process of loading, unloading, packing and disposing trash. He also made sure I did not forget anything. He checked behind me and I checked behind him. It took the mover much longer than expected to pack everything because they needed to prepare my furniture for storage vs. moving it from one home to the next. They had to wrap glass, tables, living room furniture, fragile items, etc. After reserving a storage space, purchasing a lock for the storage unit, moving supplies and an additional hour for the movers, I paid out $800 I was not expecting to spend. I tried so hard not to be stressed. Then I was reminded from Proverbs 10:22, "The blessing of the LORD, it maketh rich, and he addeth no sorrow with it." Getting approved for the new apartment was such a blessing. Then the offer from my sista friend to stay with her while I waited for my new apartment to get ready was a bonus. I could have been stressed out, but it would not have changed anything. In that moment, I took a deep breath and said, "Thank you God."

Since I spent $800 in unexpected costs, I wondered if my new apartment community would offer a concession beyond the prorated rent. I knew it would not hurt to ask. According to James 4:2, "…Yet ye have not, because ye ask not." Therefore, I called and asked. I sent an email requesting a move-in concession which was forwarded to the property manager's supervisor. After a few days, the leasing manager shared with me the supervisor declined my request for a concession. Not to mention the apartment was still not ready. I had to accept for the first time in 14 years, I was displaced. The last time I did not have a place to call my own was in 2007. This was not a good feeling. I was blessed I had a place to lay my head, but it was not my own. My sista friend was amazing. She made me feel welcome and comfortable in her home. I enjoyed her company, and her son was the sweetest. Everything was perfect and peaceful. The best part was I was able to work from home because there was reliable internet. I was also only five minutes from my parents' house if I needed anything. God truly worked things out for me. I called my leasing manager every other day. Even though things were going well where I was living, I was ready to get settled in my own place.

Each time I called my leasing manager, she reassured me she would keep me informed as soon as she heard more about the inspection. The sad reality was everyone was waiting. There were eight apartments in my building. Two tenants were transferring from different buildings. Therefore, there were 10 families waiting to move and get settled. As of Aug. 1, the leasing manager had not obtained the certificate of occupancy. For the first time since 2008, I did not have to pay rent. I was glad and grateful. On Wednesday, Aug. 3, I received the call that the inspection was complete. Within a few short days, the property obtained a certificate of occupancy,

41

and we could officially move in. Thank God! I could finally get moved in and settled. However, it was going to take more money that I did not have. My circle always shows up for me when I truly need them. Everyone knows I only ask when I really need it and this time, I really needed it.

I needed about $2,000 to move. There was one person who let me borrow $300, but everyone else gave me the money without needing to pay it back. I was truly blessed. I had everything I needed to pay rent, my security deposit, and a moving crew. My utilities were already covered and active in my name. Things were finally falling in place for me. Then I discovered I had a lingering bill from Crestmark that I had to pay in 30 days, or it would be sent to collections. When I received the closing statement from the assistant leasing manager, I was livid. There was no reason why all charges were not already billed to me back in July. Nothing she communicated to me made sense. I was very bothered. I wanted to dispute the charges, but I was tired of going back and forth. The closing statement was over $600. Therefore, in addition to my moving expense for my new apartment, I was required to satisfy a balance with Crestmark to ensure it did not impact my credit.

Without any further fight, I logged into my online portal and submitted the payment. I was glad to be officially done with Crestmark Apartments. They were at the top of my list of worse places to live. On Aug. 9, I picked up my keys and signed my lease. It was such a rewarding feeling. When I got back to my sista friend's house, I let her know I would officially be moving out in two days. Her response took me by surprise. Things had gone so well and been so peaceful that they were not ready for me to leave. It was such a humbling moment for me. I felt so welcome and that meant a lot to me. The next morning, I decided to take everything to my new apartment and get my clothes out of storage. When my sista friend came down for work and saw everything packed up she said, "I thought you were leaving on Thursday." I said, "Yes, I know, but I decided it would be easier to meet my movers from my new apartment since the storage unit was only three minutes away." I gave her a big hug and thanked her again for everything. I could not thank her enough.

My significant other and I went by my storage to pick up my clothes. He wanted to do whatever he could to help as well. I appreciated his efforts. He got all my clothes out of storage and carried all of them inside for me. Halfway through the process, he said, "You're not going to have enough space for all these clothes." I started laughing because I honestly did not feel I had a lot. Then I asked him, "Did you see the closet space?" I knew the answer but wanted him to humor me. When he brought in the next load, I opened the closet door. His eyes grew big, and he replied, "You do have enough space!" He was amazed at how large and spacious the closet really was. Not only was there enough room for my clothes, but there was space for my shoes, tubs, and miscellaneous items as well. Not to mention, my closet could also hold a washer and dryer if I decided to purchase one.

It was such a blessing having the extra closet space since I had downsized to my smallest place to date. I was grateful. When my significant other brought all the clothes inside, I was relieved. It was one less thing I had to worry about on moving day. The next morning, I prepared to move my big items out of storage. The

43

movers were scheduled to arrive by 8:30 a.m. In addition to moving, I had to go to the doctor as well. At 8 a.m., I received a call from the movers advising me they could not pick up the truck until 9 a.m. All I could do was shake my head. There was nothing else I could do. I had a tight schedule, and they were not making it easy for me at all.

I shared with them that whether they were finished or not I had to leave at 11 a.m. and whatever was not complete in two hours, I would figure it out on my own. I was not willing to pay out more money for movers. Alijah came to help me again. I was grateful he was an adult. This meant he could stay with the movers while they unloaded the remaining items when it was time for me to leave. Thankfully, before I had to leave, most of my furniture had already been unloaded. I think they realized my sense of urgency and worked to get things done in a timely fashion. Of course, when I returned home from the doctor, there were things that were not done. I did not dwell on it. My focus was getting the wifi installed so I could work from home. Unfortunately, I did not realize the time it was going to take to get my services installed. I had my own place again, but I was still staying at my sista friend's house so I could work from home. After a few days, I decided to just commute to the office to work. I called Xfinity on Aug. 11, 2022 to get internet. I was told it would have to wait until Aug. 28 for a tech to install my service.

I was disappointed and impatient. For the first time since the pandemic started in March 2020, I had to commute to the office every day for three weeks in a row. I was not happy, but I did what I had to do. Sunday, Aug. 28 could not come fast enough. I had just landed in Atlanta from Miami when I got the alert the tech had arrived at my home for my appointment. I reached out to let the tech know I was en route. When I arrived, there were two techs onsite. One tech was responsible for installing my alarm system and the other one was taking care of the internet and cable. Since I had to file a complaint with the Federal Communications Commission (FCC) against Xfinity, the corporate office sent an escalated team to assist. After speaking with over 15 representatives and spending over 10 hours on the phone over five days, a formal complaint was necessary. This was one of the last things my work sista recommended before she suddenly passed away. She told me she had to file one against AT&T. Therefore, I knew there would be some value in doing so.

Within two hours, all my services were connected and working. I could finally work from home. I was grateful I no longer had to commute to the office. I was starting to get settled in and things were going well. I was on the top level, so I did not have to worry about stomping or bumping above me. The community was very peaceful and quiet. It felt good to finally be at peace and in an affordable space. My apartment was new inside and out. I had no issues with things not working or needing to be replaced. I was intentionally making my one-bedroom apartment in Mableton work until it was time to purchase my forever home. It is essential to have a safe and peaceful place to call home.

45

CHAPTER 1 SUMMARY

In the current inflation and recession climate, it is vital that we secure affordable, safe and adequate housing. It is necessary to do research on property owners, realtors, apartment communities, and property management companies while renting to ensure you are well informed before deciding. Not everyone will have your best interest at heart. Though we spend a lot of time at work, we spend a lot of time at home as well. Therefore, we must be intentional about cultivating a space of peace. When the time comes to purchase that forever home, be sure to obtain a professional, experienced and knowledgeable realtor. Be patient. Things will not happen overnight. However, "And we know that all things work together for good to them that love God, to them who are called according to his purpose." - Romans 8:28.

CHAPTER 2: FINANCIAL TEST

As a student in high school from 1995-1999, I do not recall any financial literacy classes offered or taught at Redan High School. Maybe there were some available. I just do not remember it being a requirement for graduation. These are the types of classes that should be required. Even in 2023, financial literacy classes are not consistently offered to high school students. I obtained my first credit card as a first-year student in college. Inexperienced in how credit really worked, I assumed making the minimum payment on time each month was enough.

Since I was still living at home with my parents from 1999-2001, I did not have many bills to pay. My credit was really good. I received credit card offers in the mail every week after I received my first card. My first credit card was a Mastercard, which is considered a major card. The initial credit limit was $500. Within a brief time, my credit limit increased. During the holidays, I would go into several department stores to do my shopping for family and friends. When I would go into Macy's, JCPenney, or Rich's (before they were bought out by Macy's), I would walk in with the intent to browse and pay cash for any items I found. Well, every associate had the same question, "Would you like to apply for a credit card and save 25-30 percent off your purchase?" I liked the sound of a discount off my purchase. As a college student, I knew every single discount made a difference. Therefore, the sound of a discount was very intriguing. I was still very inexperienced about credit so I did not realize the impact numerous inquiries would have on my credit score. I discovered that every time I applied for a credit card, I received instant approval. Before I knew it, I had up to 10 credit cards. Creditors were relentless. It did not matter the number of cards I already had. I was getting more credit card offers.

Living at home with my parents was the saving grace. I had no major bills to pay like rent or utilities. Essentially, I worked to cover school costs and the credit card debt that was gradually growing. Things changed when I moved out of my parents' home. When I moved in with the person I was forced to marry, my credit took a major hit. I helped pay rent and other major expenses. I was no longer focused on my credit cards. Before my credit started to decline, we purchased a car. Since I did not have my license, we had to put the car in my partner's name. I still had my learner's permit and did not realize it mattered until that moment. I was listed as the co-signer. I figured that meant he was solely responsible for the car. I was so wrong. When we split up, I kept the car. I paid as much as I could. When something needed to be fixed, my father helped me. I never realized how much it would cost to maintain a car. I was convinced we purchased a lemon. It was a red Kia Sephia. The car was used, and we purchased it from a *buy here, pay here* car lot.

When I could no longer afford to pay the car note, I stopped making payments. Usually, a car is repossessed when payments stop. However, the car was never picked up by the company that financed the vehicle. After some time, the car no longer worked. I was not interested in investing more money in a car that was no longer serving its purpose. I eventually had a towing company take the car away. In 2008, my financial wellness began to crumble. My payroll department received an official notice from the court to garnish my wages. My first thoughts were, *What is a garnishment? Could I fight it? How would I fight it? Was this really happening? What was I going to do?*

After speaking with my payroll team, they shared with me that by law they were required to withhold a set amount each pay period until the debt was satisfied. I was devastated. *Who was garnishing my wages? Why are they doing this now? How much would be taken out of my check each pay period? How long would it take to satisfy the debt?* I quickly learned it was one of my credit card companies requesting to garnish my wages. There was absolutely nothing I could do to prevent this from happening. It was 2008, so I was not aware of my options. Therefore, I moved through the obstacle the best I could. Within six months to one year, the debt was satisfied. I was grateful this was one less debt I had to worry about. In 2000, my late Grandma Dean helped me with my credit card debt. She paid off my lowest and highest credit cards. I was very appreciative of her help. However, I discovered things were worse than I thought. I was not making a lot of money at that time, so it was difficult to pay off old debts. I was not very knowledgeable about the consequences I could face by not satisfying my debts in a timely fashion. It became a tough lesson for me to learn. Though my grandmother helped me with two credit cards and my wages were garnished for a third card, I still had outstanding debts to resolve.

In 2011, I was an underpaid front-end supervisor for Ross, an extremely popular retail store. Every single penny mattered during that time. I was a single mom maintaining a household by myself. Money was extremely tight. I received a letter from a

49

finance company regarding the car my ex-husband was the primary buyer for. It indicated a judgment had been granted by the courts to pay the remaining cost of a vehicle I no longer had. I was very confused. Several years had passed when I had the towing company pick up the car, so I did not understand the delay. *Why were they contacting me suddenly*? It did not make sense. I quickly learned the finance company was coming after me because they could not locate my ex-husband. I was livid. Again, I had several questions. *Why was I responsible for a car I was just the co-signer for? How could they make me pay for a car I no longer owned*?

I was oblivious when it came to debts, creditors, garnishments and judgments. These things were never talked about in school. I was clueless. I spoke to one of my aunts about her bankruptcy. We never had a lengthy conversation about it, but I remembered she used an attorney during that process. I asked her for the attorney's contact information. The same day, I reached out to the attorney to explain what I was dealing with. He told me he would be able to stop the judgment immediately. I provided the necessary documentation to the attorney, and he handled the rest. The next day, he emailed me paperwork he filed with the courts requesting to cease any collection efforts, as I was officially under bankruptcy protection. I was relieved. Even though I was not familiar with how bankruptcy laws worked, I was grateful at that moment for what the attorney had already done for me. This was the beginning of my financial breakthrough. Within a few days, I met with the attorney in person to go over necessary paperwork, payment for his services, and court proceedings. It was truly a lengthy and overwhelming process. After several meetings, the

50

recommendation from the attorney was to file Chapter 7 bankruptcy. Based on the remaining unpaid debt and my limited income, it was the most feasible option.

This was all new to me, so I relied on his expertise to make the best recommendations for my situation. I felt confident in his work and legal knowledge. Not to mention he was highly recommended by my aunt, which made a difference. I quickly learned the difference between Chapter 7 bankruptcy vs. Chapter 13 bankruptcy. However, I did not quite realize the tough blow my credit was taking. Filing bankruptcy was not a quick process. My initial appointment with the attorney took several hours. There was a mountain of paperwork to complete and sign. In addition, I had to complete a financial literacy course before the paperwork could be submitted to the courts. The financial literacy course was highly informative. It provided a realistic perspective on how to begin managing my finances better. This was also a course I would have appreciated in high school if it was offered.

I always thought it was suitable to just pay my bills on time each month. I was so wrong. I learned a lot during the bankruptcy process. It was a humbling experience. I discovered maxing out my credit cards severely impacted my credit score. I learned the difference between the statement closing date vs. the payment due date. I learned how having a mix of credit which includes revolving, mortgages, car loans, and personal loans was more attractive to banks and lenders. Soon I learned about utilization, and by keeping my credit usage below 30 percent, I appeared more responsible and credit worthy to lenders. In addition, I learned about credit age and the difference between hard and soft inquiries. I had no idea there was a mark placed on my credit file each time I applied for credit. I discovered all three credit bureaus did not report or record the same things. There was so much to learn. I was interested in learning it all. After a few months passed, I had to appear in court with my attorney. The purpose of the court date was to meet with my creditors. This proceeding was standard. It allowed creditors to dispute the bankruptcy. Ironically, I learned that in most cases, creditors do not attend the court proceedings. Most bankruptcies are not disputed. My case was no different. None of my creditors came to the hearing, which allowed the judge to pardon all my debts, not including student loan debt or taxes. I learned early these things cannot be discharged and must be paid.

My attorney shared with me I would have a discharge within a few months. This meant creditors were no longer able to collect any debts covered under my bankruptcy. I had a fresh start. I was grateful. I never had a lot of debt. There was just not enough income coming in to cover monthly bills and old debts too. Before my bankruptcy was discharged, I started receiving new credit card offers in the mail. *Was this common? Did they realize I was in the middle of bankruptcy, or did it matter?* Creditors were relentless. They wanted to capitalize on every opportunity they could. In addition to credit card offers, I started receiving several notifications from dealerships to purchase a new car. I did not need a new car. My current car was paid off, and I was not interested in a car payment every month.

One of the positives that came with filing bankruptcy was once it was discharged, I would not have to surrender my car because it was mine. I worked really hard to pay it off so it would not be taken from me. I still wondered why I was receiving so many offers in the mail about purchasing a car. *How did they know I filed bankruptcy? Were there really programs available to help individuals rebuild or re-establish credit?* I discovered bankruptcies were public records. Therefore, dealerships and credit card companies could obtain this information without getting it from me directly. I was very puzzled, but there was not much I could do. In July 2011, my bankruptcy was officially discharged. I was grateful for a fresh start and an opportunity to rebuild my fragile credit. If the finance company had never attempted to receive payment for a judgment they filed against me, I may not have filed bankruptcy. Nonetheless, it was time to move forward.

For a while, I did not apply for new credit. I did not pull my credit reports to determine what was listed or what my scores were. In December 2011, I decided I wanted to purchase an iPhone. I was using MetroPCS, which was a new major phone company established in 1999. MetroPCS did not offer iPhones, so I had to explore other options. MetroPCS was not the best phone company, but it worked for the time being. If I wanted an iPhone, I knew this meant I had to go with one of the larger phone companies which included: AT&T, Verizon, Sprint or T-Mobile. Though I was familiar with AT&T, I decided against that option. I went into the Apple Store to determine what was the best approach. An Apple associate advised that I would need to fill out a credit application with a phone company to get the iPhone. After spending several minutes pondering which company to choose, I selected Sprint. The anxiety I felt in that moment was vast.

53

I was incredibly nervous. The palms of my hands were very sweaty. My head was pounding. The knots in my stomach made it hard to focus. I thought to myself, *would I be denied service with Sprint? Would it be an awkward moment between me and the associates if I was not approved?* I was not sure what Sprint requirements were, but I filled out the application by providing general information to the associate, and she submitted it on her tablet. Within a few seconds, I obtained instant approval. Not to mention, I was approved for up to eight lines. I was ecstatic! I was in shock, but overly excited. *Was my credit better since my bankruptcy? Or, did Sprint have minimal requirements?* I did not overthink things or dwell on it. I finished up the necessary paperwork, picked out my iPhone, and went home. I felt accomplished. I was so hopeful at that moment.

Before long, I applied for a few credit cards. This was in an effort to further rebuild my credit post-bankruptcy. Things were going well. However, my income from working was still not enough to cover all household expenses. I constantly found myself in a hole. I was still working at Ross as the front-end supervisor. My hourly rate was $9.83. Rent in 2012 was much more affordable than it is today, but was still a major struggle for me. I was an individual living paycheck to paycheck. I could never save for my rainy-day fund because I was paying out everything I was bringing into my home. Therefore, I had to get a second job.

I started working at JR Crickets in Mableton. Since I was working full time at Ross and attending college, I had limited availability to work at JR Crickets. I was grateful the staff was willing to work with me. I became acquainted with balance quickly. I

54

desperately needed the extra income, so I did what was necessary to obtain it. For a while, having the second job worked, but I still struggled with finances. I minimized the number of credit cards I applied for, but the credit cards I did have were maxed out again. I was disappointed in myself. I knew I needed to shift things soon.

In 2014, when I started working for a major natural gas provider in Atlanta, Georgia, I finally felt like I could breathe. I was making enough money to handle my bills. I was in a good space and grateful. Things truly started to align for me. In January 2015, I moved out of my two-bedroom, one bathroom apartment into a three-bedroom, three-bathroom townhome. The approval process was seamless. I obtained instant approval. It was four years after my Chapter 7 bankruptcy, and things were turning around for me. I had no idea six days after I moved into my new place I would be buying a new car. My current car had a blown head gasket. Though my father helped me cover the cost of getting the car fixed, the car did not drive the same. Each time I got behind the wheel, I was concerned with safely making it to my destination and back. The car wasn't smooth and I needed a reliable car fast. I was still familiarizing myself with credit and inquiries. I knew applying for a car would result in several hard inquiries being added to my credit report. I did not want that. Not realizing God was already working things out in my favor, I checked my mailbox. God's timing is always perfect. He will make a way for us even when we cannot see a way. When I checked my mailbox, I had a pre-approved offer from Capital One Auto Finance. The offer was for a car loan up to $35,000. I stared at the offer for a moment. *Was this real? What was the catch? What did I have to do to take advantage of the offer?* After reading the letter and fine print several times, I put the letter aside until the next morning. When I got to work, I pulled up the website online. I provided my general information and social security number. I received a second approval for a car loan up to $35,000.

This meant Capital One would be my finance company, and I would make my car payment to them directly. All I needed to do was find a car from one of the preferred dealerships, sign the paperwork, and drive off the car lot. I was in denial. It seemed too good to be true. *Could I really select the car I wanted? Is there a catch? Was I missing the fine print?* This was never the case in the past. When I went to a *buy here, pay here* lot, based on my credit and income they selected the cars I was eligible for. I never had the option to pick the car I wanted. It was a lot to absorb. I was excited and nervous at the same time. After getting all the details from a representative at Capital One, I had planned to go to the dealership to get my car immediately after work. The time seemed to move slower than normal that day. Of course, there was nothing I could do besides wait until I could clock out. I was becoming impatient. However, the end of day was busy, which took my mind off the clock. The time finally arrived. It was 4 p.m., and I could finally go get my car. I was still nervous, but hopeful.

When I arrived, I made it clear to my sales advisor that I did not want to use any of the financing options they had available. I shared with him that I already had a pre-approval from Capital One Auto Finance, and there was no need to run my credit with any other banks. He mentioned it was standard to run the info through different lenders for the best rate. I said, "No!" I reiterated again, I have a guaranteed pre-approval with Capital One, and I was not interested in exploring other options. I did not want excessive inquiries on my credit. I stood firm on my decision to not allow the dealership to run my credit again. It was simply not necessary. I asked the sales advisor if I needed to take my business elsewhere or if they were willing to honor my request. At that point the sales advisor and manager knew I meant business and no longer pressed me about running my credit again. I test-drove a few cars and finalized my decision. I selected a 2012 Chevrolet Cruz Limited Edition. I was not picky when it came to cars. My focus was reliability more than anything else. I also wanted a car that had good gas mileage. I was confident in my choice.

When we got back to the dealership, my file was sent to underwriting. The manager told me what my monthly payments would be and that I had seven days to satisfy the $1,000 down payment. I signed my paperwork and drove home. Little did I know, I would be taking my new car back to the dealership less than 24 hours later. After I left the dealership, I knew I needed to pick up food. However, since I had the new car, I wanted to stop by the house to pick up Alijah. I wanted him to see the new car and take him for a quick ride. When we arrived at the restaurant, I thought I saw smoke coming from the hood while we were sitting in the drive-through. Wow! *Was this really happening?* I was not 100 percent sure if it was smoke from my car or not so I remained calm.

The next day, when I took the car back to the dealership, I discovered I was right. My car was smoking. It was running hot because it needed a new water pump. I was upset. I was confused. I was overwhelmingly frustrated. I could not understand why a car

57

that needed a water pump was included in the fleet of cars to sell. I did not pick my car up from the service area. It was parked on the lot with the other cars listed for sale. Though the issue was resolved in a few days, it was one of many repair trips to the dealership. It was disappointing, but I pushed through it. Buying my car was the last major purchase for a while. Things were going well financially, or so I thought. Another challenge I faced besides credit card debt was personal loan debt. Before I knew it, I had three personal loans, several credit cards, car payment, insurance, plus my monthly household obligations. The sad reality was I was still not saving any money. Though my income increased, my monthly expenses increased as well.

I never considered myself an excessive spender or shopper. It just seemed like my debt was steadily increasing. *Did I, once again, take on more than I could handle? Where did I go wrong this time? Did I take on much more than I should have?* Absolutely! *Did I make the right decisions*? Not consistently, and it was starting to catch up with me all over again. *Why was I back in the same position I found myself in seven years ago?* I was saddened to be back in that space. I felt like I let myself down. I could not continue making the same mistakes expecting different results. My fresh start was wiped out so quickly due to my poor decisions. After speaking with my bankruptcy attorney, he shared with me that I was not eligible to file Chapter 7 bankruptcy. There was a waiting period of eight years which meant I could not file a second Chapter 7 Bankruptcy until July 2019. *What was I going to do? What would be a more effective approach this time?*

58

My attorney recommended I file Chapter 13 bankruptcy instead. The difference between the two was this option created a repayment plan. The payments would be deducted from my payroll checks and sent directly to the trustee. The trustee would then disburse the payments to certain creditors. After pondering for some time regarding the current financial state I was in, it was best to move forward with the Chapter 13 filing option. I was hard on myself for a while. I held my head low and was self-critical of the negative choices I made again regarding my finances. I kept accumulating unnecessary debt.

During the Chapter 13 process, I had to surrender all my credit cards to my attorney. He mentioned the trustee would ask where my credit cards were being held. I had no intention of increasing the debt I already had. Therefore, I willingly released all credit cards to my attorney. It felt good being able to pay some debts in affordable installments. However, I was patiently waiting for the opportunity to file Chapter 7. I was at a point in my life where I was tired of struggling so badly with my finances. I was tired of making the wrong choices. I was tired of not being able to save. I was tired of being charged outrageously high interest rates. It was time for a change.

While I was actively under my Chapter 13 bankruptcy, credit card companies started sending me new offers again. I just did not understand why this happened so often. *Was the system designed to cause us to fail?* I was determined not to fail again. I tore up every credit card offer I received. It seemed like the more offers I tore up, the more I received. I was unwavering in my decision. Since I was facing another bankruptcy, I knew I would have to rebuild my

59

credit all over again. I knew I would not find myself in this position again. After receiving more credit card offers and throwing them all away, I made the decision to apply for one credit card. Just one. After obtaining approval, I vowed to consistently make the right decision. I kept my utilization below 10 percent. I made all payments on time. When new offers arrived, I disposed of them immediately.

In March 2020 during the height of the pandemic, I transitioned from Chapter 13 bankruptcy to Chapter 7. I had to complete more paperwork. I had new court dates to attend. On June 22, 2020, my final Chapter 7 bankruptcy was discharged. I tried to settle with Capital One and pay a portion of the remaining balance on the 2012 Chevy Cruze, but they declined. I sent three offers and each time they refused. I knew I needed a new car. My bankruptcy attorney was very resourceful, which is why I appreciated his role during this journey. He provided me with information about a sales specialist in Charlotte, North Carolina. I never purchased a car outside the state of Georgia, but I was encouraged based on all the wonderful reviews. I shared with the specialist my budget which was the most important thing. He sent me over a list of cars to choose from. I was overly impressed with my options. Most of the cars were newer models and had little miles. This was definitely a first for me because all my cars had 50,000 miles or more. After my close friend agreed to drive me to North Carolina to pick up the car, we collectively decided on the best day.

On July 23, 2020, officially one month after my bankruptcy was discharged, I had a new car. I purchased a 2019 Hyundai

Elantra with less than 8,000 miles. I was immensely proud. Not to mention my car insurance dropped really low as well. The sales specialist was very impressed with my credit score coming out of bankruptcy. He even asked, "How did you obtain such a high credit score coming out of bankruptcy?" I shared with him that I was actively building my credit while under my bankruptcy. I was still using one credit card and would now add my car note which would continue to boost my credit scores. Although my credit score was not as high as I wanted it to be, I was grateful for the progress I made. One month post-bankruptcy, all three credit scores were close to 700.

I promised myself at that moment I would continue to take my finances seriously. I would continue to build my credit responsibly. I would make the right choices and commit to saving. I minimized the number of credit cards I obtained. I did not apply for personal loans. I was no longer taking on more than I could handle. If I could not pay cash for it, I did not buy it. By simply changing my way of thinking first, I implemented and executed an adequate financial plan that worked for me. I committed to financial wholeness which allowed me to be mindful of spending habits. This was essential to ensure I was not excessively spending and being wasteful with the income I was bringing in. I was committed to maintaining a strict budget by reducing monthly expenses and creating a realistic savings goal. Most financial experts stress the importance of paying yourself first. By following this simple tip, it allowed me to save consistently, something I struggled with for years. It was also helpful having my savings automatically deducted from my checks. To achieve my goals, I had to change my way of thinking. I did not want my son to go through the same things I went through. I had to set an example for him. I was intentional about my son having a strong financial foundation, so I helped him build his credit. I talked to him about things he should focus on and things he should avoid. I took pride in seeing my then 18-year-old's credit score as high or higher than mine. I did not want him to make the same mistakes I did, therefore, I educated him on credit utilization, statement closing dates, due dates, credit age, and soft and hard inquiries. I wanted him to understand what it takes to be considered creditworthy.

"Each one, teach one," is a very popular quote used for an online credit repair company I follow on social media. It stresses the importance of teaching one another the things we learned that would be beneficial for others. Therefore, I continue to instruct my son so he can make informed decisions when it comes to his credit. I am willing to help as many as I can to ensure they do not make the same mistakes I made on my financial journey. I do not consider myself an expert, but I have helped and encouraged others not to make the same mistakes I made. As we get older, it is necessary to make the right decisions, especially when it comes to our finances.

CHAPTER 2 SUMMARY

Financial wholeness is essential. It ensures you are still able to maintain household bills and expenses comfortably, should an emergency occur. It is important to pay yourself first each pay period. By doing so, it helps you save effectively. If you have your savings account connected to your main checking account and this is problematic, consider a savings account that is not linked to your main checking account. Sometimes when we see our savings, the temptation is there to use it. Separating these accounts will help avoid the temptations. Obtain credit reports annually to review for accuracy. Set up credit monitoring with a reliable source such as MyFico. If you cannot afford this option, credit bureaus do offer some credit monitoring features free of charge. Remember, Credit Karma should only be used for informational purposes only. Finally, make the right decisions for you. If it sounds too good to be true, it probably is. Do your research. If all else fails, reach out to a trusted financial advisor for assistance. Take control of your financial freedom immediately!

RESILIENCE

64

When I think of family, several things come to mind. Mother. Father. Sister. Brother. Aunts. Uncles. Cousins. Nieces. Nephews. Grandmothers. Grandfathers. Foundation. Connection. Sacrifices. Patience. Selflessness. Imperfections. Grace. Forgiveness. Stability. Growth. Vulnerability. Love. Understanding. Courage. Peace. Happiness. Unity. This is what family looks like from my perspective. Family sometimes consists of individuals who are biologically connected. In some cases, family can represent individuals who are not related by blood at all. Family can be individuals who decide to demonstrate love by taking someone in as their own because there was no one else willing to do so.

Family is not always about those who have known you the longest. It is about those individuals who step in and commit to being there for you no matter what. Family includes individuals who decide to love you, support you, encourage you, and push you throughout life's journey. Family does not mean things will be perfect, easy or stress-free. It means God has equipped us with individuals within our circle to help us navigate this thing called life. In most cases, we do not get the opportunity to pick our family. God is in control. Though we cannot control our biological family, we can commit to doing our part to ensure there is a healthy and happy unit.

The mother-daughter dynamic is special, but it is not always easy. There is generally a bond that develops from birth, though this is not always the case. As a child, I cannot remember a time I did not want to be with my mother. Through the good, bad, happy

65

or sad times, I wanted to be with my mother. As a young girl growing up in my mother's single parent home, my sister and I had our share of great times, as well as struggles too. We did not always have the latest brand of clothing, expensive shoes or even designer bags. My mother kept our hair done even if she had to do it herself. There were some nights when my sister and I did not have enough food to eat, but my mother always made it work with what we had. We were young, so we never complained. We also did not want to give our mother a tough time. We felt she was doing the best she could.

Although we never wanted to give our mother a tough time, we did endure some scary moments. When my big sister and I were younger and attending elementary school, my sister was hit by a car. Everything happened so fast. I was crossing the street with my mother and walking up the sidewalk toward our home. When we discovered my sister had been hit by a car, I had several questions. *Why did my sister decide to not walk with us? Why did my mother leave her? Where was my sister when she attempted to cross the street? Was she trying to catch up with us?* I never saw what happened, but at that moment, my mother told me to go home while my sister laid on the ground yelling, "IT HURTS, IT HURTS, IT HURTS!"

My sister was transported to the hospital by ambulance. I was so scared. Even as a young child, so many questions rushed through my head. *Was my sister going to be okay? Would she be able to come home soon? Would she be able to walk again?* I was sad. I was worried. I could not recall a time when my sister and I were not together, so this was an extremely hard time for me.

Thankfully, my sister did not have to stay at the hospital long. I was grateful when she came home, but we knew she would have some recovery time.

Another scary moment my sister and I encountered was when she was being bullied by a boy at our school. It was not clear why the boy targeted her, but he would not stop. When she told our mother the boy kept picking on her, our mom made the decision to take matters into her own hands. One day after school, our mother confronted the boy, which resulted in her slapping him. No, it may not be the best decision for an adult to slap a child, but our mother did what she felt was best in that moment. The consequences of her actions resulted in a night in jail, but the boy never bothered my sister again.

I recall so many fun and loving times with my mother. She would clothe us in her dresses for holidays. One year, my sister and I were witches for Halloween. Rather than ugly witches with warts, my mother called us "pretty witches," which we were. She made our faces up with light makeup. She dressed us in her long black dresses, and we had matching witch hats. It was such a memorable moment. My sister and I did everything together. If I could not go, she could not go. If she went somewhere - even if I did not want to go - I went too. My sister and I had to share a bedroom. I would be responsible for my side, and she would be responsible for hers. That was often a challenge because I was very neat and organized. My sister was not. We would often get in trouble because our room was a mess. It had everything to do with my sister's side of the room, but it did not matter to my mother because we were in the same room. If she got in trouble about the room being a mess, I got in trouble about the room being a mess. I never thought that was fair, but I dealt with it.

Most kids who shared a room had to share a TV as well. Sharing a TV was difficult. If my sister wanted to watch something, I was out of luck. My sister was the oldest, and she used that to her advantage. We often had arguments because she felt it was fine to do whatever she wanted to do. In addition to one TV, we shared one small closet. This was where we kept our clothes and shoes. Thankfully, we had a closet in the living room I could use for some of my items. Things could have been a lot worse, so I kept a lot of my feelings to myself.

Sharing anything with my sister was definitely an adventure. It was not ideal since my sister was very bossy, but I got through it. The same was true when we moved into my father's home in 1994. I was restricted to one side of the room, and she had the other side. Though my father was not in the same household with us when we lived with our mother, he maintained a constant presence in our lives. There is not a moment in my life that I do not recall my father being there. While living with our mother, there were times when my sister and I were home alone. This was especially true when we would get home from school. Many of us experienced life as latch-key kids. This meant we used a key to let ourselves in the house after school. We were instructed to stay inside and lock the door until an adult got home. My sister would immediately feel like she was in charge. She liked to boss me around. I knew it was her way of keeping me safe, but it was annoying.

RESILIENCE

One day, my sister and I were walking home from the school bus. When we walked around the last corner before we got to our house, we experienced a shocking discovery. There was a lot of furniture, clothes, shoes, and household items in the front yard. Kids were going through the items, taking what they wanted, and saying mean things. Girls were laughing. Boys were making jokes. One boy said, "Look at all this junk in the front yard." It caused all the other kids to laugh hysterically. The closer we got to the house, it did not take long for my sister and me to realize it was our things sitting outside. It was not clear what my sister was thinking, but her expression went from sad, to worried, to mad in a matter of seconds. I even recall her yelling at the kids to leave our things alone and hearing them laugh even harder.

I was confused and truly oblivious to what was happening. We went to the door and realized we could not go inside. *Where was our mother? Did she know what was going on? What were my sister and I supposed to do? Where should we go? Who should we call?* While my sister and I stood there unsure of what we should do, our mother pulled up with one of her friends. My sister instantly asked what was going on. She had a way of asking questions at the wrong time. My mother was obviously embarrassed and trying to gather what she could. She screamed at my sister and told us to go to my grandmother's house. Due to the stress my mother was clearly under, I did not ask any more questions. I gathered what I could and headed to my grandmother's house with my sister. It was not a short trip, but it was not a long trip either. There were so many thoughts running through my head, so I could only imagine how my sister was feeling. We later discovered we had been evicted.

When we arrived safely at my grandmother's house, she was glad to see us, but she had a lot to say. She was disappointed at our current circumstances. We were officially without a place to call our own. After some time passed, I began to worry about my mother. She had not made it to my grandmother's house with the rest of our things. None of us knew where she was. I started to worry. *Was she okay? Was she still trying to gather things from our old house? Where was she going to put our things?* Little did I know at that time, it would be a few days before I would see my mother.

My grandmother shared her insight and highly recommended that we go live with our dad. I was not ready to leave my mother. I was hopeful that whatever was going on with her, it would get better. However, the ugly truth was we did not have a place to call our own. We were occupying space in my grandmother's home. It was such a complicated time for us. My sister and I were 12 and 13 years old. We had never experienced such a traumatic event like this before. It took some time to process it all. Nevertheless, my sister felt excited at the thought of moving in with our dad. Actually, she wasted no time gathering the few things she had and moved in with him.

It was the first time I had been separated from my sister. I was sad. I felt alone. For the first time in my young life, I felt abandoned. Thankfully, my grandmother allowed me to stay in her home until I made the decision to go live with our dad, too. Within a few days, my mother arrived at my grandmother's house. I was so grateful and relieved she was okay. She extended several

70

apologies for what we were going through. As expected, she was embarrassed and ashamed. If my sister and I felt embarrassed, the level of embarrassment my mother felt was even greater.

I still had hope and believed things would get better. Unfortunately, things did not get better. My mother was not able to secure a new place for us to live. This meant we remained under my grandmother's roof longer than she expected. However, the home had plenty of space. There were four bedrooms on the main level, a large room upstairs with the attic, and a full basement downstairs. The only downside was we only had one bathroom. The home was typically full. In addition to my grandmother, some of my aunts and uncles lived there as well. There was never a dull moment - especially when my uncle lived there - but my grandmother was strong. She handled things the only way she knew how. No matter how hectic things got from time to time, it was home. Besides, I was simply appreciative that my grandmother allowed me to stay until I moved with my dad in January 1994.

When I moved to my dad's house, things were different. We had strict rules to follow. Deviating from these rules meant severe consequences would follow. My sister and I had a consistent church routine. We were in church every Wednesday, Friday, Sunday morning, and Sunday night. We had several revivals, shut-ins, consecration service every weeknight in January, and our convocation every September. We were members of the choir and usher board, and we actively participated in our women's fellowship meetings and events. We also had stability. We were officially in a two-parent home. My Dad married my bonus mom in 1988. My oldest brother went into the Navy, and my baby brother

71

was in preschool. The one thing that remained unchanged was my sister and I shared a room. Of course, she was in her feelings about having to share a room with me after having a room to herself, but there was nothing either one of us could do.

Moving in with my dad meant I would attend a new school. I was excited to do so but worried about the individuals I would encounter. I was at the end of my 7th grade year when I moved in with my dad. At my previous middle school, I was bullied, and I fought a lot. I was ashamed by the number of times I was suspended for fighting. I never realized fighting at the bus stop in your neighborhood would cause the school to suspend you for fighting. I experienced that. I often wondered who reported back to our administrators that there was a fight, but never knew. Again, living with my mother, I did not have name brand clothes or shoes, which is why I never understood why folks bothered me. I was very quiet, shy, and stayed to myself.

Thankfully, with the new school, I did not have any significant issues. I knew better than to try my dad. He would not be as understanding as my mother was when it came to fighting. My dad held us to high standards, and I did not want to disappoint him. I made new friends quickly. It was encouraging to have friends who lived in the same neighborhood. I was not allowed to go outside much, but we were able to walk to and from the bus stop together.

One of my best friends for over 20+ years until she passed away in 2017, TT, lived in the same neighborhood as me. We did a lot together. When I could visit her home, we had so much fun. We listened to music, walked to the store, and watched movies. Her mom did my hair and cooked dinner. I met all her siblings, and she met mine. TT and I were always together. We did not have any classes together, but when we saw each other throughout the day, it was always an exciting time.

Another best friend I met in 7th grade was LM. She was very popular. Everyone knew and loved her. She was so down to earth and real. I truly appreciated someone who was as authentic, honest and friendly as she was. We had a few classes together, and it was always a great time. The year ended quickly. I had to say goodbye to most of my friends for the summer. Of course, I would not see my friends who did not live in the neighborhood until school started again in August.

I was grateful the summer was quite eventful for my sister and me. With our weekly church schedule, there was always something to do. My grandfather made sure the church had several picnics and fishing trips. It was very enjoyable to spend time with my church family, cousins, and any friends who we could invite with us. We also took family trips every year. This was a new experience for my sister and me. Any time we had the opportunity to travel outside of Georgia, it was a blessing. We always had so much fun. I remember lots of trips to Orlando, which included visiting Disney World and Universal Studios. The U.S. Space & Rocket Center in Alabama was also a fun experience. I really appreciated the exposure to these places. My parents were intentional about creating memories.

In addition to summer trips with the family, we also experienced many family reunions. My bonus mom has roots in Athens, Georgia so that is where many family reunions were held.

Athens was also the resting place for my bonus mom's mom. Therefore, we had an opportunity to visit her gravesite while we were there. We often held our family reunions the weekend of Mother's Day, so the timing was very fitting. I have so many wonderful memories of spending time with my family during the summer. The summer came and went very quickly. After the family trip, church events, and family reunion, it was time to go back to school.

My 8th and 9th grade experiences went by pretty quickly. Redan High School was so crowded, I shared a locker with someone in my homeroom as a first-year student. In addition to sharing lockers, the hallways were overcrowded, and it was difficult getting from one side of the school to the other between classes. It was quite an adventure. I made every effort to adjust to high school the best I could. I was grateful some of my friends from middle school went with me to high school. My grades were pretty decent too. In 10th grade, my dad allowed me to try out for the JV Drill Dance Team. I was very nervous. I had no prior dance experience, but I had rhythm. I also enjoyed dancing on my own time. We had a clinic Monday-Thursday where we learned and practiced a new routine. Then on Friday, we had try-outs. When it was time to do my routine, I was so scared. My heart was pounding so hard, I thought I was going to pass out. My hands were shaking, and so many things were running through my head at that moment. This was my first time performing a routine to be considered for a team. I was very nervous, but hopeful. I gave it my all, and got through the routine pretty quickly. I made sure I smiled and gave lots of energy. When I finished, I packed up my things and went home. Later that evening, I received a call from another student who tried out with me. Some of the other students who tried out stayed until the names were posted. When she called to let me know I made the team, I was ecstatic! I was very proud of myself. I did it.

After weekly practices and the first performance, my coach named another student and me co-captains. It was such a surreal moment. Not only did I try out for a team and make it, but I was also selected to be a captain as well. This opportunity meant the world to me. It made me feel like I was doing something right. I was selected as one of the captains because I had proven to my coach that I was one of the best on the team. It meant I had a reputation to uphold. I was a leader of a small group of my peers, and it was quite a humbling moment. My time on the drill team was very rewarding. It taught me how to work and perform on a team. It showed me how working hard pays off. It also taught me to never give up. I was not ready for the season to end, and I convinced myself to try out for the varsity drill team my junior year.

While living in my dad's household, we had to maintain suitable grades. I took pride in doing well because I realized my grades were a reflection of me. Since my dad allowed me to participate in extracurricular activities, it was important for me to keep my grades high. I did not want to give my dad any reason not to let me participate. At the end of my sophomore year, the varsity drill team had clinic and tryouts for the upcoming school year. I wanted to be on the varsity drill team so badly. However, I was afraid. The routine we had to perform for tryouts was much harder than JV tryouts, and it was longer. There were more stunts and moves to execute. Not to mention, I was intimidated by all the

75

veterans trying out for a spot. I thought to myself, *Do I really stand a chance? What should I do? What will they say if I do not make it?* My mind was racing. I went to the clinic each day and gave it my all. The day of tryouts, I went to school in my tryout clothes so I would be prepared. Most of the veterans saw me around school and knew I was trying to make the team. They were like big sisters to me and very supportive. As the end of the school day came faster than normal, I allowed the fear of potentially not making the team prevent me from even trying out. I was very disappointed in myself, and to my surprise, so many others were disappointed as well.

For the next few days, I had several individuals ask, "Why did you come to school dressed like you were going to try out, but did not show up?" I was so embarrassed. All I could say was I changed my mind at the last minute. Instead of being on the varsity drill team as I aspired to do, I ended up being one of the managers for the entire auxiliary (drill team, flag corps, and majorettes). That meant whenever they had a performance, I was there helping to lighten the load for the coaches and sponsors. Whenever we had a game, parade, competition or exhibition, I was there. I also assisted the band as well. I served as a chaperone when the ladies needed to go to the restroom. I helped with pre-game prep by ensuring the ladies had everything they needed and more. I even added glitter to their makeup before each game and/or performance. I really enjoyed being with the ladies each week. We became extremely close.

The band was invited to Mardi Gras in Louisiana. It was such an exciting time because most of us had not been to Mardi Gras before. Of course, there was a cost associated with the trip, but I wanted to go. When I asked my dad if I could go, he said no! I had never traveled anywhere without my family, so I knew this time would be difficult. I was not happy about being told I could not travel with the auxiliary and band to Mardi Gras. A few weeks later, I received my report card. I had all A's and one B. I recall my entire family being very proud of me. I was proud of the efforts I made as well. When I showed Grandmother Dean my grades, she was extremely impressed. I could not remember if I spoke to her about the trip, but she provided her insight. When we were leaving church, my grandmother asked my dad, "What are you going to do for this girl making these good grades?" My dad just shrugged his shoulders and said he did not know.

The deadline for the trip payment was rapidly approaching. My dad had not changed his mind, and I had not mentioned it again. One morning when I was preparing to leave the house for school, my dad came into the living room. Typically, I did not see my parents when I would leave for school, but I did acknowledge my dad when I was leaving. That morning, he came into the living room and asked if it was too late to make the payment for the trip. I was so excited that he was going to let me go on the trip. Honestly, I was not sure if it was too late to pay or not, but I shared with my dad that if the deadline had passed, I would bring the payment back home. When I got to school that morning, I rushed to the band room. I learned the deadline had not passed, and I was right on time. That made me very happy. I could not believe my dad was letting me go on a trip without my family. I was overjoyed.

In addition to trying out for the drill team, my dad allowed me to take Driver's Education Class in high school. This was a big deal for me because none of my other siblings had the opportunity. My sister had a few challenges with her grades, so she was not given the opportunity to participate in any extracurricular activities, including driver's education. When I first moved in with my dad, my sister kept losing her house key. Each time the key was lost, my dad changed the locks. He wanted us to prove to him that we were responsible. When he agreed to let me take driver's education, I believed he thought I was responsible. Taking driver's education meant I needed to get my learner's license. Obtaining a learner's license meant I would practice driving with an adult. I let my nerves get the best of me again. I aced the simulation, range, and classroom portion of my driver's education course. However, I struggled badly on the road. When I drove with my instructor, I did well when it came to the basics, obeying all stop signs, traffic lights, and adhering to the speed limit. When it came to turning left, I had some challenges. Every time I took my road exam, I failed. To this day, I do not know why my confidence in driving was not stronger as a 15-year-old. Maybe it was because I was still so inexperienced. Most evenings after church, my father took me out to practice driving, but that was not enough. Needless to say, Driver's Education was the only class I failed in my entire educational journey. If I had passed the road test, my overall grade would have been 96 percent. After several failed attempts on the road test, I ended the course with a 69 percent. I was very disappointed in myself. At the time, I wondered if I would ever learn how to drive well enough to get my regular license. There were so many thoughts running through my head, but my father was supportive through it all.

78

Living with my father meant I had his love and support up close and personal. Let me be clear, my father has always supported us. Of course, it was from separate homes since we lived with our mother previously. It never changed the fact that he was an active part of our lives. I enjoyed being able to experience life with my father. Things were not always easy, but it made us closer. For that, I am forever grateful.

On November 28, 1989, my baby brother was born. He changed all our lives for the better. He took over my role as the baby of the family, but I would not change it for the world. I enjoyed being able to go to my father's house on Sundays to see and play with my baby brother. He was the cutest little baby with so much hair. We loved him and spoiled him. He was the favorite for sure. He received lots of attention. My brother ended up being my closest sibling. We just seemed to relate to one another a lot more than my other two siblings. After high school, he left home to attend college. He was accepted into Tennessee State University and was in the marching band. Every chance I could, I traveled to Nashville to visit him. Tennessee State University Homecoming was always a popular time to visit. We had so much fun and always had our brother-sister talks. He also supports me 110 percent when it comes to Alijah. Whenever I need him to simply have a conversation with my son, he is always willing to do so. There was a time when my brother purchased a bus ticket for Alijah to visit him in Nashville. I was very grateful for the gesture. It meant the world to me that he was willing to take time with my son. It truly does take a village. As a single mom, I needed all the support I could get from the men in my circle. My brother has always been supportive. I knew his authentic love and support of others would serve him well in his role as a father.

On July 28, 2017, exactly three days before my father's birthday, my baby brother had his first child, a precious baby boy. He was the third of the Scott clan and officially the one tasked with carrying the legacy on. It was such a proud moment. I was officially an auntie to a baby boy. I vowed to show up and be a part of his life as much as I could. Though I did not make it to Nashville for his birth, I have traveled each year since to celebrate his birthday. It is a joy watching him grow into the smart little boy he is becoming. He has big shoes to fill as he is carrying my father's and his father's name. We have no doubt he will carry on the legacy well.

In September 2020 in the midst of a pandemic, my baby brother got married. It was such a beautiful weekend for our family despite the limitations and restrictions due to Covid-19. We all came together to celebrate the union in the midst of it all. My oldest brother and his family came down from Virginia, and everyone else traveled from Georgia. Typically, we all have separate accommodations, but this time we had one big Airbnb. Everyone stayed together, and there were no major issues. It was such a blessing to be there to support my brother. Everything went well, and I was grateful to be a part of a major milestone in his life. He had grown up right before my eyes and was now a married man with a child of his own. It was surreal. My nephew and his cousin were the ring bearers for the wedding. It was such a joy seeing him participate in that major moment. My nephew is very smart and is a great big brother. In addition to my nephew, my brother and sister-n-love had twins - a boy and a girl. Again, another

80

opportunity to give God praise! Since my brother and his family are outside of Georgia, there are not many opportunities for us to all get together. When those opportunities present themselves, we try to capitalize on those moments.

My niece, who lives in Virginia, played basketball throughout high school. In March 2021, the basketball tournament was held in Gatlinburg, Tennessee. My father came up with the best idea. To support my niece, he developed a family trip where everyone who could travel would drive to Gatlinburg. Since Gatlinburg was one of my favorite places to visit, I was excited for the new family trip. My bonus mom, father, sister, son and I traveled from Atlanta. My baby brother and his family traveled from Nashville, Tennessee. Of course, my oldest brother and his family traveled from Virginia. It was great to have all the kids and grandkids together. It was such a blessing to spend time and make memories together.

There were definitely a few hiccups, but we got through them all. My sister and I were at odds because she likes sleeping with lights on and I do not. My son had a major dispute with my oldest brother based on a conversation we were having collectively as a family. However, after a serious conversation with my baby brother, things were peaceful again. There continued to be small disagreements throughout the time we were together, but no family is perfect. Things will not always be peaceful. However, we learn to make the best of each situation and grow from the experiences. Though we went through a few tough moments, March 2021 was when I discovered my baby brother and sister-n-love were expecting another baby. I was honored to be one of the first to receive the news of the new addition. Also, I had the opportunity to spend time with my nephew and niece. I do not get the opportunity to spend time with them often because we all live in different states. Therefore, I wanted to make the best of each trip with my family. We played games, ate breakfast and dinner together, went to the water park or pool, and played miniature golf. We had so much fun. These are the moments I live for. In the midst of the hard times, God was still faithful. I was intentional about doing what I could to be a part of it all. I wanted my father to be proud of the sacrifices I was willing to make to be with the family. I vowed from our first trip to make each trip thereafter better than before.

In 2022, I created an agenda for that year's gathering so everyone would know what we had planned each day. I took pictures from our first trip and added them to the agenda. I felt the pictures added a special touch and served as a reminder of the memories we made the year prior. It was a small gesture, but my father was very appreciative. I made sure to include a morning prayer, a Scripture, game night, breakfast or brunch, and dinner. These activities created memorable moments for our family. It warmed my heart to see the smile on my father's face each year.

In July 2023, after several years of not hosting a family reunion, my oldest brother and baby brother, along with a few cousins, decided it was time to revisit our annual family reunion. In an effort to ensure everyone was included and informed, communication regarding the family reunion was sent via email. The communication was effective and provided an opportunity for everyone to participate if they wanted to do so. Individuals were able to select items to bring or donate to ensure one person was not responsible for doing everything alone. The family reunion turned out to be a great success. Those who were supposed to be a part of the reunion were there.

It was peaceful. It was fun. It was entertaining. It was encouraging to see the next generation take the lead and execute a memorable event in a way our parents and grandparents would be proud of. There was a lot of food, drinks, cakes, cookies and games. It was very hot. Thankfully, we had a pavilion to sit under. There was also a water pad that kept the kids cool and comfortable despite the heat. By the end of the day, we were all a few shades darker, but it was well worth it all.

No matter the good, bad, happy, sad, proud, frustrating, rewarding, disappointing or challenging times, family is all we have. Since we technically do not get to choose our family, we must make the best of what God has blessed us with. It is essential for us to cherish the moments while we can. Life, it seems, is getting shorter and time is too precious to waste. Love on the members of your family the way God wants us to do.

83

CHAPTER 3 SUMMARY

Family, one of the most important gifts God has blessed us with, should not be taken lightly. Though family may not consist of individuals related by blood in each scenario, it is the connection that makes people family. No matter how the family was developed, it is important to treat the ones who make up your family right. Cherish those who you hold near and dear to your heart. Be intentional about making memories. We only have one opportunity to do this thing called life, so we must make each moment count. If someone in the family has done wrong by you, talk it out and work through the problem. Remember, God forgives us, so we must forgive those who may not do right by us. When you make the decision to forgive, be sure to let it go. Family is one of the most important things God has blessed us with. Do your part to keep the family together. If everyone collectively does their part, the family can remain a happy and healthy unit.

CHAPTER 4: RELATIONSHIP TEST PART II

In February 2021, there was a major shift in my relationship with DE. DE is the man I met in 2019 through social media. We were connected in so many ways and things just felt different with him. It was authentic. I felt loved, valued and appreciated. I really loved this man. The truth is, I was in love with him. He came into my life and took my whole heart. It was refreshing, yet scary. We were consistently and regularly spending time together. We were creating memories and loving on each other the way a healthy couple should. This was truly a pivotal moment for me because my love language is quality time. The simplest, most valuable thing DE could give me was quality time.

At that point in our relationship, he was doing well in his efforts. I was truly grateful. I never wanted to feel stagnant in any area of my life, especially my relationships. This relationship was no different. If we were not growing and glowing together as a unit, I did not want it. It was important that DE and I were in sync with one another. Initially, one of the key things that attracted me to DE was his faith in God.

It was essential for me to have a man who believed in God the way I did. Someone who was comfortable praying with me and praying for me was vital. I am a strong believer of being equally yoked together. The Bible tells us in 2 Corinthians 6:14, "Be ye not unequally yoked together with unbelievers: for what fellowship hath righteousness with unrighteousness? And what communion hath light with darkness?" Therefore, it was substantial for me to be equally yoked with DE.

It was not enough for us just to have similar likes, dislikes, goals, passions and aspirations. It was necessary for us to have the same beliefs and values relating to spirituality. I prayed for this relationship to work. I prayed for this relationship to be my last. However, the sad reality is things do not always fall into place or go the way we envisioned. Trusting God through the process is important even when it is not easy. There were some tough lessons I had to learn while cultivating a relationship with DE. Some lessons were harder than others. Other lessons were hurtful. Many lessons were essential for growth. Still, there are some lessons I am currently learning.

As I mentioned previously, February 2021 set the tone for my relationship with DE. Things seemed to be going very well for us. After a very serious conversation, DE and I decided to start a new business venture together. He was already in the home renovation business and doing very well. He was just working with a business partner. The home renovation industry was something he was truly passionate about. I enjoyed seeing him execute in his role as a contractor and boss. It brought him so much joy, which made me feel happy.

He called me one afternoon and said, "Baby we need to start our own home renovation business." Since this was his passion that I supported 110 percent, I asked, "*What do we need to do to make this happen?*" Serving as the operations manager for a successful massage business, I was very familiar with the paperwork process, license requirements, requesting an Employer Identification Number (EIN), obtaining insurance, and registering with the State of Georgia. I was just not sure how soon he wanted to embark on this journey. I found out very soon just how serious he was. He was adamant about getting this done as soon as possible.

It was still unclear why he had a sense of urgency, but before we concluded the call, he made it known. He said to me in the sincerest tone, "I am tired of doing all the work and having to split things in half. I do not want to make millions with anyone else but you." I was extremely humbled. I had a man in my life who loved me and was intentional about including me in every aspect of his life. He made sure I felt included in the decisions he wanted to make for us. I greatly appreciated that. As we discussed the logistics for starting a business, we collectively decided on a name - DSE Home Renovations LLC. I was proud of how well we worked together to get things done. I completed the paperwork. He covered the fees. He made suggestions. I completed necessary research. We worked as a team to get things done, and I enjoyed that feeling. It was those small moments that mattered the most to me. The fact that he valued my opinion about things made me feel included. I appreciated that. This was different, and it felt amazing.

At that moment, it never crossed my mind how the current business partner would feel about the change. However, I found out sooner than I wanted to. After a lengthy but productive phone conversation, DE and I made substantial progress starting our business. We obtained the EIN from the Internal Revenue Service. We submitted the business name to the Secretary of State for approval. We set up the State of Georgia tax account. We started working on the paperwork to obtain a business license from the City of Atlanta. There was so much to do. We were executing the process very well. On February 9, 2021, DE and I received our approval for the business formation. It was such a rewarding feeling.

The enemy has a way of creating distractions during the worst times. Things were falling into place seamlessly as we started the business. Then, things started happening with DE which impacted us. At the beginning of March 2021, DE and I were texting back and forth, which we typically do during the day while we are working. His father was in town, and he was making the most of their time together. I was grateful he had the opportunity to fly his father into town to spend time with him. After a few messages back and forth, he mentioned he was frustrated. I immediately wanted to know why, so I asked. After a few moments, he told me his account was frozen. My first question was, *"What account was frozen?"* My second question was, *"Why was the account frozen, and how long would it take to be unfrozen?"*

I knew that was not a good situation to be in. I could only imagine what DE was feeling at that moment. Frustration did not even begin to scratch the surface. Soon I found out just how impactful having a frozen account was. The most disheartening aspect of the situation was that the business partner was in complete control. She made it seem like the account was undergoing an audit and that no one would have access to the accounts until it was complete. I did not know this individual personally. I knew she was someone DE had to set strict boundaries with to ensure things remained professional. It was evident their time working together had generated feelings. However, DE was

88

intentional about making it known he was in a serious relationship, and he would not allow anyone to impact that.

He was extremely professional when it came to handling business. I also realized this individual was someone DE trusted. Unfortunately for DE, days went by, and there was no communication from the business partner. Days turned to weeks. Weeks turned into a month, and DE still did not have access to his funds in the business account he shared with the business partner. Thankfully, DE had funds available in his personal account that he could use until the issue was resolved. Neither one of us knew how long the audit would take. The business partner was not as forthcoming with information as we needed, but this was just the beginning of the nightmare we would experience with this individual. Though we were grateful DE had a backup account with finances available, those funds were not being replaced.

Not only was there a freeze on the account, but DE was not able to accept any new jobs. He needed funds to accept new jobs and approve bids. Upon approval of bids, materials and supplies were needed as well. In addition, other contractors were needed to assist with the job, which meant we had to hire and pay those individuals. With most of DE's assets being frozen, he experienced substantial strain in his day-to-day operations. The most frustrating thing about the situation was that an individual he trusted demonstrated she could not be trusted. She was not communicating as much as she needed to, and DE was not asking the questions I would have asked over and over again until I received a suitable answer.

89

DE and I had no idea things were going to get worse before they got better. A week after learning his account was frozen, he was faced with yet another challenge. On March 17, 2021, I received a phone call from DE in the middle of the day. Typically, because we are both working during the day, we do not call each other. As I mentioned, we communicate via text. I felt something in my spirit that did not feel right. As soon as I answered the phone, I asked him what was wrong. He asked what I was doing. My braider had just started to braid my hair. I let him know I was getting my hair done and it would be a few hours. As soon as she was finished, I called him right back. He did not answer.

When I got to the car, he texted and asked if I was done with my hair. I said yes. I could still feel something was wrong, but he was not saying much. He asked me to meet him, so I did. I assumed he would be in his truck, but he took a car service to meet me instead. When he got in the car with me, he mentioned he needed to get some food. So, we discussed food options. Once we determined what he would eat, there was a brief silence. A few moments later he said to me, "Someone stole my truck." I was completely blown away. I was speechless for about two seconds before I had a series of questions. I was shocked. I was annoyed. I was upset. I felt like the enemy was truly attacking him. A week prior, he learned his account that he shares with his business partner was frozen due to an audit. Now, he was dealing with not having a vehicle.

I was hurt. I was disappointed. I had so many questions. I asked, *"When was the car stolen? From where was the car stolen? Did the police provide any updates yet?"* I know he probably felt

90

interrogated, but I had the passion of a lawyer inside me. He let me know the car was stolen a few days prior. He was out at a lounge in Ellenwood, Georgia. When DE discovered his truck was gone, there was no evidence it was broken into. You may typically find broken glass on the ground when someone breaks into a car. This was not the case. DE also had both keys to the truck with him, so the individual who took the truck did not take it using the keys. Things were not adding up.

After we picked up food, we went back to my house. He stayed with me, and we just enjoyed being with one another. The first opportunity I got, I gave him the tightest and longest hug. We stood in the middle of the floor in silence. I knew he was hurting. I knew he was upset. There were too many things happening at one time. Even the strongest can only handle so much before it becomes overwhelming. I did not like seeing him in this space. I did what I could as his woman to pour into him through the storm. I tried not to ask a lot of questions, but I wanted to know what was going on. Men like to deal with things on their own, no matter how much support is provided to them. I knew this season was going to take a lot of patience for both of us.

During the day when I worked exclusively from home, my car did not move. I knew DE had things he needed to handle, and being able to get around was essential. Therefore, I allowed him to use my car to run errands. Since DE thrived on being a very independent man, it was difficult for him to accept help from anyone, especially coming from his woman. He was appreciative and expressed authentic gratitude. It was just a difficult time for

91

him. I understood. Through the storms, we had to keep going. It was hard, but we kept fighting.

Since 2021 was a milestone birthday for me, I wanted to go somewhere I had never been before. I wanted my birthday to be memorable. I was so grateful to be a few months away from Chapter 40. To help DE focus on something positive, I told him I wanted to go to Cancun for my birthday. He instantly asked, "How much does it cost?" I was tickled. I mentioned that if we were serious about taking the trip, he needed to get a passport. I did not realize the mountains I would have to climb to make things come together.

I learned quickly that DE did not have a copy of his birth certificate. We were definitely going to need that to apply for his passport. I immediately started researching how to obtain his birth certificate since we would have to get it from New York. Once I obtained that information, I told DE I needed a copy of his identification. He attempted to send it via text so I could print it, but that did not work. After a few failed attempts, I shared with DE we would have to meet in person to get this done. As I prepared to leave town for a family trip, DE and I met at Office Max to copy his ID and to fax it to the organization helping us obtain his birth certificate. Thankfully, that process went smoothly, and his request was approved. Since we expedited the delivery of his birth certificate, we received it in record timing. I ordered two copies, just in case he lost one. I was grateful things were falling into place for DE to obtain his passport.

Since I recalled having such a seamless process at the post office in downtown Atlanta, I suggested to DE we go there to complete his paperwork. When we arrived one weekday morning prior to opening, there was a long line outside. DE saw it and instantly said, "No, we are not doing this." Some men just do not have patience. DE is one of them. It did not matter that I completed the passport paperwork for him. He wanted me to take his picture and present the documents to the agent too. It was hilarious. I told him I understood he did not want to wait, but we needed to get it done as soon as possible. We finally agreed to go back later that day, but we never made it back to the post office that day.

I asked DE every other day when we were going back to the post office. I knew I had to stay on top of this if we stood a chance of getting his passport in time. One evening before closing, we went back to the post office. There was no line outside, so we were encouraged. When we checked in, the clerk advised us it would be at least two hours. DE was not having it. I took a deep breath and said, "We have to get this done." He looked at me and said, "I need to eat." I told him we would eat as soon as we finished with the process. Almost two hours later, his number was called. Thankfully, I had already completed the paperwork, so that part of the process was done. All we needed to do was get his picture taken and pay the fee. We had to have his passport expedited to ensure we received it before our trip. Since our flights and accommodations were already booked and paid for, it was essential we received his passport timely. When we finished up at the post office, we picked up food, and went home. Despite what DE was going through, he remained positive.

At the end of March 2021, DE took me on a date. I was so excited because it was officially our first date. Yes, we had eaten together several times, but at that point, we had not eaten out together. Typically, we would cook at his house or mine or get take out from a restaurant. That moment was very special for me. DE was still going through a storm, yet he made time for me. This meant so much. He took me to dinner at a nice Mexican restaurant. It was special because he planned it all. It was also a place I had never been before. We talked. We laughed. We flirted with each other. We plotted. We planned. He took care of me and made sure I received whatever I wanted and needed. We really enjoyed one another.

It was so refreshing and what we both needed. It was at that moment I realized just how much DE loved me. In the midst of the storm, he was still thinking about me. He was still thinking about us. He was going through things but planning for our future. I loved that. I did not want to bring up the situation with his business account being frozen or not having a vehicle, but he wanted to let me know what he knew. At that time, he expected the audit to be complete in a few more weeks. He was confident. He was encouraged. It made us feel better that he was in a good space about the situation.

After a week or so passed, I asked him if he had heard the latest from his business partner. Instantly, I knew something was wrong. His response was, "She's a snake." I thought to myself, "*Uh oh, what happened?*" DE let me know the business partner was no longer communicating with him and that there were now thousands of dollars missing from the business account. I had so many questions. I could feel the anger building up inside of me. *What type of audit was the account under? Who was conducting*

94

we got dressed and headed out. Our resort was in the hotel zone, but to get to certain places we had to take public transportation. Our concierge specialist kept us informed. He reassured us that taking the bus was inexpensive and safe. When DE and I got dressed, we headed to the bus stop where several folks waited. The bus arrived shortly after. DE and I were not sure where we wanted to go, but we got off the bus at Hard Rock Café. There were folks everywhere. It was truly a vibe. DE and I walked around a little bit before going into Fat Tuesday. Every restaurant and bar were packed to capacity. Luckily, we found an empty table with two chairs. We ordered drinks and vibed with the music blasting from the speakers.

There were bottle girls. There were guys selling tickets for a raffle. There were women offering henna tattoos, as well as hand painting. Since it was almost my birthday, I decided to get my hand painted. It was unique and creative. The paint also glowed in the dark. After a second round of drinks, DE started talking to a few of the workers at Fat Tuesday. He told me he would be right back. Not long after he left, I started missing him. *Where was he? Why did he leave me? Where did he go?* Places were starting to close because it was getting late. Even though we were pretty close to our resort, we had to take the bus to get back. When folks started leaving, I became worried. DE had not returned.

I walked around trying to find him. I noticed one of the guys I saw him talking to. I tried to ask him if he knew where DE was, but he could not understand my English. His first language was Spanish, and I took French in school. The knots in my stomach were growing. I was worried. I had no idea where DE was. I was still stuck on the fact that he left me by myself in another country. This was not good. This was bad. *What was I going to do? What was I going to tell his sister?* She was his emergency contact, and she really cared about her brother. I was in full panic mode. I took out my phone and called 9-1-1. I was so scared. I did not know what else to do. Calling 9-1-1 did not help. The operator spoked Spanish and did not comprehend what I was saying. I was over it. At that moment I was worried and upset. After being very close to tears, DE walked around the corner. The first words out my mouth was, *"Where have you been?* I was so worried about you!"* He explained he was trying to find a store to replenish his cigarettes. Though it was an epic fail, I was grateful he found his way back to me. I thought to myself, all of this chaos over cigarettes. I was in disbelief.

I was upset with him for walking away and leaving me alone, but I was so relieved to see him. I held on to him for dear life. After I told him how scared I was and that I called the police, we shared a laugh. It wasn't funny at all, but he understood my worry. We waited for the bus back to the resort. When the bus arrived, we grabbed a seat and he fell asleep. When we arrived at the resort, I woke him up because he was still sleeping. My King was tired. Plus, we had quite an adventure and it was very late. Once in our room, we showered and slept. The next day, my Birthday eve, things didn't go well. DE and I had a misunderstanding which resulted in us spending the afternoon apart. He spent the day at the pool. I got a massage. After my massage, I went back to our room to shower. Shortly after, I rode the bus into town. He checked on me to make sure I was safe, but it was disappointing not spending the day together.

100

home, I pulled into the driveway. The driveway is where I typically parked when I visited his home. However, the garage door was opened, and he told me to pull inside. Wow, this was the first time he asked me to park in the garage. *Was he worried about my well-being? What was going on now?* At that moment, I realized DE was on high alert as well. A few hours later, I was preparing to leave DE's home when we both spotted an unusual SUV. It was parked in front of his neighbor's home but close enough to DE's driveway. *Was this woman following me? Was she stalking DE? Was this really happening?* I made it home safely that evening. I communicated with DE the moment I got in the house. We were both on edge for each other because we had no idea what she was capable of.

A few days later, we discovered she knew DE and I started a new home renovation business. She texted him a screenshot of our business formation paperwork from the Georgia Secretary of State. In addition, she now had my home address because we used my info to register the business. The following week, I added a Xfinity alarm system at my home. We were not willing to take any chances with an individual who did not appear to be stable. Things were a mess. DE could not sell his home due to the latest appeal filing, and now we had to be concerned with being followed. It was just too much.

In June 2022, DE received a call from one of his ex-business partner's acquaintances. Obviously, they led him to believe that if he could convince her DE and I were not in a relationship, she would cancel the appeal. I was extremely upset. *What did our relationship have to do with any of this? Why did he have to convince his ex-business partner we were not together? Why did we have to lie about our relationship? Why did we have to deny a relationship we had been cultivating since 2020? Did she really think she still had a chance with DE after all the chaos she caused? Was this woman serious?* None of this made sense to me. I wanted DE to be able to sell his home and bounce back from all the madness, but not at the cost of damaging our relationship. I was blown away that this was even a consideration. *If we went along with this foolishness, what would it prove? What else would she want from DE in the future? Would the agreement to drop the lien be recorded? What proof did we have that, if we entertained this, she would keep her word?* I knew there was a lot at stake. I was very angry because, once again, a woman who should have been a non-factor had all the power and control. Weeks passed and there was still no mention of the appeal being dropped or DE being able to sell his home. The anger that built up inside of me was substantial. At times, I knew sacrifices had to be made, but they had to be beneficial. It had to make sense. None of this made sense to me. DE and I struggled badly after this. He tried to reassure me he had things under control.

I knew DE meant well. I knew he loved me. I knew he cared about me and was extremely protective of me. The sad reality was DE was desperate. He was desperate to make things happen so that he could get things back on track. Sadly, it did not happen the way he anticipated. 2022 ended and we were both praying for a fresh start. DE and I were attempting to regroup from the challenges we endured in 2022, but it was not easy.

As we embarked on 2023, I was hopeful. I believed things would fall into place for DE, and I would conquer several things I had in store. There were a lot of milestones happening in 2023 that I was looking forward to. My tutoring business, Marci's Creative Nspirations LLC, was turning 10 years old. DE was turning 40 years old. DSE Home Renovations LLC was turning two years old. Among other things. I was anticipating all the things God had in store for me.

In March 2023, after almost three years together, I broke up with DE. I planned a romantic night for the two of us, and he did not show up. Hurt and disappointed, I ended things. At that moment, I felt like DE had an inability to put me first. *Was I overreacting? Did I take things to the extreme? Did I think things through clearly before making this decision?* I never gave DE an opportunity to explain why he did not make it. I just felt he should have communicated with me no matter what. I always considered DE my forever, so this break up was difficult. I did not break up with him because he cheated on me or treated me badly. I broke up with him out of hurt and anger. I had valid reasons for my decisions, but it did not make it any easier. After the breakup, I did not talk to DE for over two months. Thankfully, life for me is busy so I had several things to do to keep my mind off of the breakup. In May 2023, DE had a major health scare. He was still the man I loved, so I was very concerned about him. In June 2023, shortly after his 40th Birthday, he had to get a procedure done. I was grateful to God he made a way when we could not see a way. The things DE was going through drew us together again. We never discussed getting back together. I just wanted to be there for him as a friend.

RESILIENCE

In August 2023, I decided it was time to cut household costs by eliminating cable. I started with Xfinity in 2010, which meant I had cable for 13 years. I never watched TV that much, so I was basically throwing money away. After I purchased Firesticks from Amazon, I felt it was time to release my boxes back to Xfinity. Removing the box from the cable cord in the living room was seamless. However, my bedroom cable box was a bit stubborn. I told DE I needed his help, and he dropped what he was doing to come help me. I was very pleased and grateful for his help. Whenever I needed something and he was available, he came to assist. DE and I started spending a lot of time together. It was good to see he had bounced back from the difficult years he endured. I loved that for him. I always wanted the best for DE. It had not changed since we broke up. By October 2023, DE and I were telling each other that we loved one another again. Though DE and Alijah experienced a disagreement in October 2021, they became cordial with each other again. Whenever I needed something, it was clear I could count on DE, and he could count on me. It felt good having him in my life again. It was important for me to take things slow. However, I was open to whatever the future held for us. The fact remains that I love him, and he loves me. I am a firm believer that what is meant to be, will be.

CHAPTER 4 SUMMARY

Relationships take work. Everyone must be willing to do their part to help cultivate the relationship. It is essential to adequately communicate, especially when there are disagreements. Remember to be respectful. Be mindful of one another's feelings. Keep family and friends out of your relationships, especially marriages. You must be willing to put in work. Every day will not be perfect. Take time apart if necessary. Things worth having are worth fighting for. What is meant to be, will be. Do not hold on to toxicity, disrespect or abuse. These things are non-negotiable. Never forget your worth. When a relationship is no longer serving you, be bold enough to walk away.

110

CHAPTER 5: FRIENDSHIP TEST

My interpretation of friendship is a solid connection between two or more individuals who have established a healthy and happy bond between each other. Friendship is defined as *the state of being friends*. To establish friendship, there must be trust and support between individuals. I consider a friend as someone who I have spent time getting to know and developing a mutual bond. I met my very first friend at Mary Lin Elementary School in Atlanta, Georgia. We connected immediately and always spent time together. We always ate lunch together, played at recess, and spent time together at home. She was so sweet and friendly. She was easy to get along with, and we had several things in common. I think it is very true when people say children do not see color. My very first friend was not African American. She was Caucasian. The color of our skin did not matter. We had a pure and innocent friendship that I valued at a young age.

I wanted to be the same friend to others as they were to me. In elementary school, creating happy and healthy friendships was seamless. We were young and coming into our own. We were not competing with one another, stabbing each other in the back, or being jealous or envious. We just wanted someone to play with and talk to during school. When we moved back in with my grandmother, my sister and I had to change schools. I was not happy about leaving my best friend. It was such a difficult time for me, and it created instant sadness.

111

RESILIENCE

I wondered if I would ever meet someone as sweet and kind as she was, and I did. Shakia Guest-Holloway was another individual who became my best friend at an early age. She was so sweet and quiet. Her spirit was sincere and pure. Not only did we have class together, but we walked home together too. It was such a rewarding feeling having a new best friend. I was grateful to God for bringing a new friend into my life. Thankfully, some of the friends I grew up with in elementary school are still present in my life today. Shakia is one of them.

In middle school, it was not as easy to develop healthy friendships. I endured several challenges. When I was in 6th grade, I attended Sammye E. Coan Middle School in east Atlanta, Georgia. I do not recall having one single friend. I experienced bullying and jealousy from my peers. I was suspended for fighting several times. I was so afraid of a girl who kept bullying me that I took a knife to school every day.

The bullying happened on the school bus each morning. The bully always made fun of me and said mean things. Thankfully, when I was in school, I never saw her. One day when we were on the bus, she asked me, "If I slap you, what are you going to do?" Since I was very shy and quiet, I never said much. When she asked the question, I simply responded, "Nothing." As the fear built up inside me, I wanted to know what would possess this girl to bully me. I had never done anything to anyone. I kept to myself. I never treated people badly. *Why was I a target?* I did not have name brand clothes, shoes or bags. I was the product of a single parent household with a limited income. Besides, in 6th grade, I did not

112

focus on how I looked. I just made sure my clothes matched and I smelled good.

I guess I zoned out or she did not hear my response, so she asked the question again, "If I slap you, what are you going to do?" Again, I repeated, "Nothing." I was so scared that I sat very quietly and still in my seat. I was stuck. The fear of the unknown is a tough position to be in. In that moment, the unknown was getting the best of me. I thought to myself, *what was next? What was she going to do?*

A few moments before we arrived at school, she slapped me hard across my face and burst out laughing. Sadly, she was not the only person laughing at me. A few others laughed as well. I was shocked that she could be so cruel to slap me for no reason. I was hurt. My blood was boiling. I was humiliated. I was angry. All I could think about was going home to my mother and telling her what happened, but I never told her. I never told anyone. I was embarrassed. I sat quietly in my seat.

When we arrived at school, I got off the bus and went to my first class. I never mentioned what happened to anyone at school. I wanted to get through the day and go home. The following morning, before I left the house for school, I walked into the kitchen and grabbed a knife. I was mad. I felt it was time to protect myself. I was not concerned about the consequences of my actions. I had to deal with a bully picking on me every day and someone who was bold enough to slap me for no reason. I was not thinking about someone finding the knife. The type of knife I had in my jacket pocket was a steak knife we all use in our kitchens. I was smart enough to know a butter knife was not going to get the job

113

done. I wanted her to suffer the way she hurt me. If she bothered me again, there would be consequences. Each day, I added an extra knife to my jacket pocket because I did not know what she was going to do. *Was she upset with me about something? Was she jealous? Or, was she just that evil?* I had at least four knives in my pocket at one time, so I was ready. I was going to make sure she never bullied or bothered me again. Even then, God was looking out for me because I never experienced bullying from her again. She never looked at me. She never talked to me. She never picked on me again. She never put her hands on me again. I was grateful for God's protection. I knew there would be severe consequences for me if I had to use the knives or if I was caught with them. Even worse, there would have been severe or even fatal consequences for her if she had continued to bully me. I thank God for keeping me safe during it all.

I was not this person. I did not intentionally hurt people. When I got into a fight, it was not because I started it. It was always due to someone bothering me. Or someone who was jealous of me or what they thought I had. In some cases, it was due to people testing my patience to see just how far I would go. Taking knives to school every day to ensure I felt safe was very dangerous. Yet, it did not stop me from doing what I felt was best to protect myself. The sad reality is I never mentioned what I was going through with anyone, not my mother, big sister, or grandmother. Honestly, I do not know why I kept what I was going through to myself, but it taught me a valuable lesson. I am not alone, even if I feel alone.

Shortly after the bully encounter, I made the decision to move in with my father. I was going to miss being with my mother.

However, I needed a fresh start. Besides, my sister was already living with my father and things seemed to be going well for her. I did not need a perfect life. I just needed one with less complications. In January 1994, my father enrolled me in Miller Grove Junior High School in Stone Mountain, Georgia. It was the first time since elementary school that I could admit to having friends again.

My late best friend, TTB, was my very first friend when I moved in with my father. She and I lived in the same neighborhood. These were the best friends to have. A person I could walk to and from the bus stop with. Someone who was there to talk to me about everything and a person who would listen when an ear was needed. TTB and I did so much together. I spent time at her home often. We walked to the store together. Her mom did my hair from time to time. We ate dinner together. There were times when we took professional pictures together.

We were always laughing and having fun. TTB was the life of the party. Her energy was infectious. I loved her so much. From Miller Grove to Redan, we were inseparable. She went into the military after high school, so we lost touch. However, in 2010 when I created a Facebook page, I reconnected with all those I missed and wanted to get in touch with, including TTB. I was grateful to connect with my best friend again. We kept in touch as much as possible. When she was in town, we always talked but did not have an opportunity to see one another in person. TTB was officially home from the military, and I knew we would finally get together. Even though we talked about getting together often, we never did. Not too long after TTB got home, she decided to go back into the

115

military. We never talked about why she made the decision to go back, but I felt like there was nothing else she wanted to do. I authentically supported my friends, and TTB was no different. I showed her that if she needed me, I would be there.

In November 2017, while scrolling through my timeline on Facebook, I saw several classmates expressing their hurt and offering their condolences with pictures of TTB. My heart dropped. I was confused and wondered what was going on. *Why were people posting pictures of my best friend all over social media? Why were they offering condolences? What happened?* I went to her Facebook page where several people had posted similar messages. I was still in denial because not everything you see on social media is accurate. I needed information from the source. I called TTB from the last known number I had for her. No answer. I sent a message via Messenger on Facebook. I received no response. I was still not willing to accept what was going on.

I was close to TTB's siblings as well because I would see them in her house when we were growing up. I reached out to her baby brother to find out what was going on. I asked him not to tell me TTB was gone, but he did. He confirmed she passed away the night before. He shared with me my best friend since 1994, of over 20 years, committed suicide. I burst into tears. I was heartbroken. I was distraught. He continued to tell me she reached out to someone the same day, letting them know she was not in a good space, but that individual just brushed her off. I was crushed. She was crying out for help, but no one was there for her. It truly allowed me to put things in perspective. It let me know it was still necessary to check on individuals even if they say they're okay.

116

The passing of TTB was such a difficult time for me. She passed two short weeks after I lost my grandfather. It was such a hard pill to swallow. I was grateful for her brother keeping me informed about things. I was very sad when he shared with me TTB would not be laid to rest in Atlanta, but in Ohio. The timing was bad, and I could not leave Atlanta. I was numb. I was sad. Losing a best friend is extremely hard. Imagine the heartbreak I endured not being able to see her and say my final goodbyes. I was devastated. In that moment, I was grateful to God for bringing her into my life for more than 23 years. I will never forget her.

I was blessed to obtain a few close friends while attending Miller Grove. LaShonda Morris, better known to her friends and family as LaDae, is a gem. She is beautiful inside and out. She was very popular in school and commanded attention in any room she walked into. She is authentic. I appreciated her for her transparency. We had an instant connection and got along well. She is such a beautiful spirit. LaDae and I had minimal time together during school. After we finished middle school, she moved away and could not go to Redan High School with most of us. It was hard not having her with me, but we found each other again as adults. We picked up where we left off. It was rewarding to connect with a best friend from childhood in my adult years. LaDae has always supported me and cheered me on in everything I have ever decided to do. It means the world to me. I believe in holding on to friendships that bring value to my life. LaDae has always added value to my life, and I know the feeling is mutual.

Sadly, not all friendships are meant to last forever. The truth is, we outgrow friendships like we outgrow the clothes we wear.

117

Instead of holding on to friendships that no longer serve us, it is best to let them go. As previously mentioned, in 2010 I joined Facebook. The sole purpose was to reconnect and find classmates I lost contact with after high school. It was such a success. It allowed me to gain a closer friendship with some people who I was not as close to during high school. It allowed me to build new meaningful and impactful friendships. In addition, I was able to enhance the close friendships I cultivated while in high school. It was quite rewarding.

There was one relationship I truly valued. I treated this individual with the utmost respect, care and support. I always showed up for every event she invited me to. I went to baby showers, children's birthday celebrations, ladies' night events, and wedding festivities. I showed up for it all. In addition, I never attended events empty handed. I always came bearing gifts, even though my presence was more than enough. I have always authentically supported individuals inside or outside my circle. It was no different with her. I was grateful for the closeness we developed post high school. She was very informative and shared a wealth of knowledge. I felt extremely blessed to have this person in my life. I truly believed she was genuine and sincere. If I was dealing with a situation - good or bad - she was one of those individuals I knew I could talk to. She was someone I believed I could trust. I found peace and joy in confiding in her. The things we discussed were kept between us. I valued that.

In 2013, when I graduated from Kennesaw State University, I planned, hosted and funded a graduation party. I invited over 75 people including this individual from high school. I was expecting a big crowd to help celebrate this milestone in my life, but I was highly disappointed. Out of the 75 invitations sent, maybe 20 people showed up. I was heartbroken. I cried. I was disappointed. The one person I expected to show up for me did not.

I wish I had received the same support I gave to others. It made me question if my events were just not important or popular enough. When the individual did not show up or communicate why, I was disappointed, but I did not hold it against her. Several individuals sent their RSVP but did not show up. I did have a higher expectation for her, but experience taught me to use wisdom. In 2017, I started hosting small intimate events with a few women in my circle. It was usually never more than five women at a time. Since I knew these women would always support me, they were the only women I invited. My success with folks supporting me authentically had not been great. Therefore, having a small and consistent group of women was a more successful approach.

The events I planned and hosted provided an opportunity for the mother, wife, business owner, employee, sister, daughter, auntie, and/or niece to get out, catch up and take a break from the norm. It provided a safe place to talk, laugh, pray, joke, vent, plan and unwind. Typically, I rented a suite or penthouse suite at the Marriott. Some events took place at my home. I would choose a theme/color and have food, drinks, games, activities, and party favors. Everyone would have such a great time, so I started hosting these events annually. I planned, hosted and funded each event on my own. After a few events, I hired my friend from high school to make party favors, punch, and chocolate covered strawberries. She was very passionate about these things, and I was never

119

disappointed with her work. Whatever price she invoiced me, I paid it without hesitation. I asked if she could attend a few of the parties. Usually when I provided the date for when the items were needed, she had other plans, which meant she could not attend. I learned to be okay with that. Even though she was unable to attend, she could always accommodate my orders. As time moved on, I always hired her to prepare my party favors, but I stopped extending the invitation.

I honestly did not think it was necessary to invite her due to the constant schedule conflict. Despite the lack of support from this individual, it did not stop me from showing up and supporting her at all the events she invited me to. One day when we were planning for an event, she said, "You never invite me to your events." Surprised, I thought for a moment and responded, "Most times you have other events to attend or a schedule conflict, so I did not think it was necessary to extend an invitation." Maybe I was wrong in the way I thought about things and should have invited her. It just made sense to me not to invite someone who was never available. I did share with her that she was welcome to attend my events any time she was available and wanted to come.

In March 2021, I hosted a Ladies Day Party at my home. It was in honor of my journey to 40, which was three short months away. As with all my previous events, I reached out to determine if she could assist with my party favors, strawberries and punch. I was excited that she was able to assist. I shared with her the color and theme. She executed my vision well. In June 2021, after a rocky start to Chapter 40, I reached out to chat about some challenges I was experiencing. To my surprise there was no response. This was unusual, but I did not dwell on it. A few days later, I reached out again. This time I received a response, but it was not what I was expecting.

She said it was unclear to her what role she played in my life. I was very confused. *What was she talking about? Where did this come from?* As the conversation continued, she mentioned how she was bothered by my outreach when things were not going so well but did not invite her to my latest event. What event was she referring to? I had not hosted an event since March 2021. Then, I figured it out. One of my sista friends held a Ladies Night event at Slush Atlanta. She placed an open invitation on social media. In addition, she sent communication via text messages. The day of the event, it rained in Atlanta, so she considered canceling it. I asked her, *"When did we start canceling events due to the rain?"* We had a good laugh about it. There were a few ladies who still wanted to go despite the rain, so we decided on a time and met at the location.

As the first round of drinks were ordered, the purpose of the event shifted. It was no longer just a ladies night event. It turned out to be a celebration for my 40th birthday. It was very unexpected for me. These ladies showered me with so much love. I was truly grateful and humbled. These women poured into me positively. Each one showered me with encouragement and support. They covered my food, drinks and dessert. Not to mention, they had the DJ announce my name and shout me out for the rest of the night. It was such an amazing vibe!

I had to explain to this individual that it was not my event to invite her to. However, an open invitation was extended to

121

anyone who wanted to attend. I reiterated to her the value she held in my life, but I quickly discovered it was not enough. I attempted to clear the air by asking if we could get together for brunch or dinner to talk. She never took me up on my offer. I sent messages to check in, and most times, there was no response, so I stopped reaching out. In high school it mattered if someone spoke to me or not because I was still finding myself. As a 40-year-old woman, it did not matter who spoke to me or who wanted to be my friend. I had more important things to deal with.

I reached out one final time in September 2021 for her 40th birthday. Surprisingly, she did respond with a simple, "Thank you." That was good enough for me. I moved forward realizing that this friendship was over. Since I left high school, I have not worried about who likes or dislikes me. We are all grown now, so I do not seek validation from anyone, especially from those who are no longer a factor in my life. Losing a close friend is tough, but the hard reality is some people are not meant to remain in our lives forever. Some come into our lives for a reason. Some individuals come into our lives for a season. Then there are individuals who God has placed in our lives for a lifetime. I am grateful for each instance God has allowed me to grow through.

Another friendship that comes to mind is one with my closest friend, Karen J. We met in middle school, and she has remained an integral part of my life even now. I have tutored her kids, attended events, and supported her through difficult times. She has done the same. She is truly a gem. She is always there when I simply need someone to talk to without judgment. I continue to cultivate this relationship because it brings value to my life. Katrina

B. is another individual who has been a supportive friend. Not only is she supportive, but she is authentic and a pleasure to connect with. We met in middle school and had mutual friends. Even though we were not best friends in school, we have become very close since that time. I had the pleasure of being invited to her destination wedding in Jamaica. It was my first time out of the country in 2019, and it was such an amazing experience. I was truly honored to be a part of such a milestone moment in her life. When we lost TTB, we were both devastated. TTB and Katrina were very close friends. If you saw TTB, you saw Katrina and vice versa. I valued the relationship they had and never tried to compete. I knew what we both meant to TTB, and there was no reason for us to compete against one another. There are times when women are envious of other relationships, which result in unnecessary challenges. I learned very early that not every relationship is meant to be the same, and I was content with that. Katrina and I have connected on a few occasions for brunch or dinner, and it is always a wonderful time. I am confident we can discuss anything with one another and not worry about it being shared. She never judged. We may not talk for weeks at a time, but our connection is stronger than ever when we do.

CJ is another person I truly value and treasure. We did not have the opportunity to connect on a personal level in high school. However, she is someone I have grown fond of since that time. In my efforts to reconnect with individuals from high school through Facebook, I was blessed to get to know her on a more personal level. CJ and I were on similar fitness journeys, so we had the opportunity to train with some of the same personal trainers. It was so inspiring seeing her conquer her goals while dealing with the trials of life. She dealt with the loss of her brother and a very close friend, but she did not give up. She kept fighting. She kept tackling her goals. She continued to make a positive impact on those around her. She quickly became someone who motivated me and pushed me to keep fighting no matter what trials may come. I am grateful to have her in my life.

There are several women in my circle that I am truly grateful for. KB and KD are two women I became closer to after high school as well. We have always had an authentic connection. We talk about anything. We push and support each other authentically. We spend time together on solo outings or events with the kids. It is never a dull moment.

LD is a childhood friend I did not know I needed. Her mom and my grandmother were very close, so with that friendship we developed our own close relationship. When I spent time with my grandmother on the weekends, she would visit as well. We had so much fun. We would always get into trouble with my grandfather. It did not matter. We made memories no matter what. Eventually, LD and her family moved from Georgia, and it was difficult to accept. Not having her in Georgia anymore was a tough pill to swallow, but there were times when she made it back to visit. The visits were not always on the happiest terms, but we made the best of it. When my grandmother passed away in 2013, we were both equally devastated. There was no way she was going to miss the opportunity to say her final goodbyes. She flew to Georgia to offer her love and support to our entire family. It meant everything to us just having her in Georgia during that time. We shed many tears during that weekend, but we pulled through it together. A year later in 2014, when I graduated with my second degree, she flew into town to celebrate and support me. She made it clear she would not miss the opportunity to celebrate me on such an amazing accomplishment. I was extremely grateful. LD is still a vital part of my life, and neither one of us will have it any other way.

Thankfully, school was not the only place I made quality friends. I have created several meaningful relationships with those I worked with. In addition, I met a lot of wonderful women from Alijah's school connections who have become friends or sisters. In my current role as a supervisor, I have met several women who have made a lasting impact on my life. Some of these ladies include TS, LM, SG, AD, VW, HG, CM, LT, RB and MW. These women have collectively supported me, poured into me positively, and have provided a voice of reason when I was going through personal or professional challenges. They have all encouraged me authentically. These are individuals who I believe will always be a support system, even when my time ends in my current role. I am truly appreciative of their love and support.

KC and RS are two women I am extremely grateful to have in my life. KC and I met while our kids were in the high school marching band. That relationship took off on a high level. God gives us exactly what we need when we need it. KC is very sweet, transparent, encouraging, supportive, positive and honest. She is always there for me when I simply need someone to talk to. She is also there for me when I need a listening ear. We can laugh, cry, pray, and get over our hurt together. She has truly become one of my forever sisters. We have taken several trips together with the band. We had the opportunity to travel on a ladies trip to Miami, and we had a blast. Having genuine individuals in your life is so necessary. I do not take it for granted. I know if there is anything I ever need, KC will be there to support in any way she can.

RS and I went to undergraduate school together at Atlanta Metropolitan State College in 2010. We took a required College Seminar class together. It did not take us long to gravitate toward one another and build a strong and powerful friendship. RS and I did not communicate regularly once we graduated from school, but we did keep in touch. I assisted her sister and niece with planning her baby shower. In addition, I supported her when she held the 1st birthday party for her son. It was always a great time when we got together.

In June 2022, we planned a brunch outing at Ponce City Market. We had an amazing time celebrating her birthday. We decided we would start getting together regularly and we did. In July 2022, after being temporarily displaced, she offered me a place to live in her home. I mentioned her in a previous chapter. My apartment pre-leased my unit and refused to allow me any additional time. My new apartment was still being built and was not ready for move-in. RS was very gracious in allowing me to stay in her home until my apartment was ready. It was such a heartfelt gesture. Typically, when individuals live together, it can damage the relationship. For us, we became closer. We had such a great connection. It was authentic. It was seamless. When I moved into my place, it was bittersweet. Neither she nor her son wanted to see me go. That meant everything to me. We both vowed it would not take us a long time to get together again, and we kept our word.

We started planning outings every month, either solo or with her son. We played miniature golf at Puttshack Atlanta. We had a bowling party with her oldest sister at Bowlero Atlantic Station. We always had a blast. To remain consistent, we started a ladies night sleepover event held at her home each month. We always stay up late talking, laughing, doing hair, and having our fruity drinks because we are both lightweight drinkers. We simply enjoy each other's company. I would not change anything about the bond we have developed. It means a lot to me.

AA and TB are two sisters I did not know I needed until God brought each of them into my life. AA is a sister I met on Facebook. She was instantly a joy to connect with and very authentic. I love her boldness and transparency. She is a published author and has well-written books. I support her because I believe in her purpose and could truly relate to her journey. I never imagined meeting someone who I would become so close with over social media. That is what the goodness of God looks like. He brought AA into my life and she has poured into me, prayed for me, and encouraged me as the big sister who never stopped believing in me. I love her so much.

TB, best known to me as my little sister, is the best make-up artist I have ever had and the only person who I trust to do my makeup. She is simply phenomenal. I love her so much for so many reasons. She has encouraged and supported me in many ways. I have reciprocated those efforts because that is what authentic friends do. She pushes me out of my comfort zone and genuinely wants to see me win. I cannot count the number of times she has helped me prepare for numerous photo shoots, weekly events, birthday celebrations, book releases, trips out of town by air or car, and so much more. She was there to help me prepare when no one else was available. In addition to ensuring that my makeup is always flawless, she helps with my hair as well. Not only is she responsible for my glam efforts, but she also supports me in my day-to-day life as well. She is always encouraging me to go after the things I want without hesitation. She is always rooting for me. I am extremely grateful for the value she adds to my life all around. I do not take it lightly, and she knows it.

Next - TS, CW and AH. These ladies have been a part of my life for a very, very, long time. TS and I met in college. CW and I grew up in church as little girls and quickly became best friends. AH and I met in middle school. TS and I instantly had a connection, and not long after, she became family. I chose her to be one of my son's godmothers, and she has not been able to get rid of me since. We have been there for one another through marriages, separations, the birth of children, new jobs, loss of jobs, loss of family members, and her decision to move back home to New York. We have been there for each other through it all. Whenever she could, she would fly out to Atlanta to see me. Whenever I needed to get away, I would fly out to Maryland to see her. She has supported me through it all. She is one of the people who offered me a safe place to stay when I was dealing with the physical abuse from my ex-husband. She served as the babysitter for Alijah when I had to work. For every degree I obtained, she sent her support and admiration. For my first published book, she flew into town for my book release event. The love she has shown has made a difference, and I am so grateful. TS is more than my sister. She is family. Her family is my

128

family, and my family is hers. Not every encounter is the best between us, but we work through things like grown women should. We talk it out and seek to gain a clear understanding of each other to move forward. I love her so much, and I know she loves me.

CW, my beautiful best friend from church has been a constant presence in my life for many, many, many years. She has supported me through the good, bad, happy and sad times. She always showed up for me when others did not. She is also one of Alijah's godmothers. Whenever I needed to talk, laugh, or cry, CW was always someone I could count on. Our closeness, connection and sisterhood mean so much to me. I am confident in knowing that if I need something, she has my back and vice versa. I love her so much and that will never change.

AH is someone I met in middle school, but we were not as close as we are now. I realize that God brings individuals into our lives at the right time, during the right season. This is especially true for us. No matter what I was doing, she supported me passionately and authentically; 100 percent. She did not waiver in her efforts to be a positive and supportive sister. I really value her for her free spirit and individuality. I can talk to her about anything. I am looking forward to building a lasting and long sisterhood with her for years to come.

I am so grateful for the circle of women I have in my life. It is not always easy to maintain a network of women and cultivate a healthy and stress-free space, but I am doing it. I am extremely thankful for the friendships I have nurtured. I enjoy building meaningful and lasting relationships through sisterhood. Some of the women in my circle have been a part of my life for many years.

There are some who have only been a part of my life for a short period of time, but they have added substantial value to my life. I am humbled and appreciative.

In 2022, I reached out to one of my sista friends and shared with her via text that I was considering starting a non-profit organization. God placed it on my heart to birth a network of women who were willing to support one another passionately and positively. Even though I had a few women who were there to support me authentically, having just a few more would have made a greater impact on my life. In August 2023, God placed it on my heart again to birth this new organization. Often, we allow fear to keep us from doing the things God has asked us to do. *Why was I dragging my feet on this? What was I afraid of?* I would share the ideas with my network of sisters, but I was hesitant to act on it.

In November 2023, while monitoring my author page on Instagram, I discovered a post from a celebrity who recently established the exact same idea. "Wow," I thought to myself. "God, I hear you." At that moment, I was convinced. I made the decision to stop being disobedient and to birth what God told me to do over a year ago. I added a task to my Google calendar, and I went to work. Before long, I had a solid name for the organization - S.I.S., which stands for Selebrating in Sisterhood LLC. Of course, being an English major, it is not ideal to have words spelled incorrectly in my organization name, but I am not concerned about the misspelling. I wanted to spell "celebrate" with an "S," so I did.

I created my vision and purpose. I decided on colors for a logo and worked with a graphic designer to execute my idea. I determined the organization would initially be membership-based and that the support would come from membership fees, sponsors, and donors. The organization would accept girls from ages 12-18 as little sistas who would be a part of the mentor program for S.I.S. The purpose of the S.I.S. organization is to create a premier network of women who positively influence the world through service, celebration and support. The mission is to authentically equip, empower and encourage women through service, support and celebration. I submitted the formation and filed with the Georgia Secretary of State on Friday, December 1, 2023. On Friday, December 8, 2023, I received confirmation that my business had officially been formed in the state of Georgia.

I applied for an EIN with the IRS and set up a professional email address. I knew I needed a business bank account. So, I started exploring the best options for the business. It did not take me long to decide on PNC Bank. They truly made the process seamless. Things were coming together the way I needed them to and I was extremely grateful. A reminder that I have for myself as I approach a new season in my life is, when God tells me to do something, I need to be obedient and do it. Things will align the way they need to because he is leading and guiding me through it all. After birthing the S.I.S. organization and in preparation for its official launch, I held brief info-session to share information about the organization. I was grateful for the individuals who not only attended and asked questions, but for those who wanted to sign up as well. Since the organization is membership-based, I created a six-question membership form. An individual interested in joining must complete the membership form. The data collected from the membership form was used to determine if an individual was the right fit. This is currently the most efficient process. As the organization grows, the process will change to align with the needs of the business. Nothing I do is for show. I am in a space of allowing God to use me to fulfill the passions and talents he has given to me. No matter how small S.I.S is currently, the most important factors are the individuals who authentically support me. I know God has great things in store for me and the women in my circle. I am embracing it all. I am grateful for it all.

CHAPTER 5 SUMMARY

As we go through this life, we will encounter and create friendships that are for a season, reason or lifetime. One of the most important factors is knowing when to let go of a friendship that no longer adds value to your life. Knowing when to regroup to save the friendship, or to continue cultivating the friendship because it is healthy, is key as well. Friendships should not be one-sided. If you are nurturing a friendship that seems like you are doing all the work, it is time to have a conversation with that individual. If changes are not made, it may be time to respectfully cut ties. Friendships are sometimes relationships we did not know we needed. Having a network of positive, supportive, authentic women is vital. Be the supportive sista friend to others that you request them to be to you. Be intentional about cultivating happy and healthy friendships. Please understand, no relationship is perfect, but when individuals are willing to work together to build or improve relationships, it makes a difference.

ACKNOWLEDGMENTS

First and foremost, I must acknowledge my heavenly Father, Jesus, for leading and guiding me on this journey again. I am so grateful for your grace and mercy. Thank you for giving me the strength when I wanted to give up. I cannot thank you enough.

To the Love of my heart, thank you for the love, support, talks, laughs, cries, and tough and rewarding times. I am thankful for where we are at this moment. I love you.

Lisa King DeJesus, there are never enough words to convey just how much I appreciate your guidance throughout this journey. It is always your encouragement that pushes me to keep going even when I want to give up. I cannot thank you enough.

Laquita Moore, thank you for being the addition to my life I did not know I needed. It was your encouragement, authentic words, positivity, and kindness that gave me the push to keep going. It was your request for a second book that gave me the motivation to get it done. I cannot thank you enough, SIS.

RESILIENCE

134

RESILIENCE
AUTHOR BIOGRAPHY

An Atlanta native, Sheirra Marci is an inspiring, enthusiastic and authentic author sharing her life experiences to help motivate, educate and heal her audience. Her passion for writing has fueled this desire to share meaningful blessings she has encountered, in addition to powerful life lessons she has learned. After publishing her first book, "Perseverance: A Reflection of Pain, Passion, and Purpose" in 2021, Sheirra Marci discovered that her story made such a positive impact on her audience, they immediately requested more. Many individuals shared how relatable her experiences were and how her journey allowed them to grow and make tough decisions they were afraid to make. Eager to give her audience more, she decided it was time to offer another transparent installment to her three-part project, "Resilience: A Moment to Reflect, Restore, and Renew." There was no better way

135

to further demonstrate perseverance, than by sharing how resilient she has been over the years.

Since obtaining her Doctor of Education degree, Sheirra Marci has focused on offering high quality educational services through her small business, Marci's Creative Nspirations LLC. She provides traditional tutoring services, prepares students for standardized testing, and assists graduate students with their studies. As she approaches 11 years in business and highly rated on Google, Marci's Creative Nspirations LLC continues to grow and thrive. This is an accomplishment she is very proud of.

Dedicated to empowering and encouraging like-minded women, Sheirra Marci launched the SIS Organization (Selebrating in Sisterhood LLC). A membership-based organization that focuses on selebrating, serving and supporting each other through sisterhood, SIS provides a powerful network of sisters that so many women are seeking. In addition, the SIS Organization offers a mentorship program for girls aged 12-18 to ensure they have the additional support and resources they need to move though life from preteen to adult in a positive and impactful manner.

Sheirra Marci is truly grateful and excited for the journey God has placed her on, and she does not take it lightly. Life is a journey, and though it is not always easy, she leans on her faith to lead, guide and strengthen her. She believes everyone should be intentional about living life on purpose. Therefore, on this journey she will continue to show up for her family, friends, King, students, parents, sista circle, and the SIS organization. We only have one opportunity to live this thing called life and she wants to leave a lasting stamp on the world while she can.

136

Milton Keynes UK
Ingram Content Group UK Ltd.
UKHW030244190324
439698UK00014B/815